The Holiest Bible Ever: Being God

Almighty God

ISBN: 1511737174
ISBN-13: 978-1511737173

EDITOR'S NOTE

Not all of this version of events is coherent or chronological (unlike fairytales, for example). That is because this is a true story, a written recording of exactly what happened, not like fiction. Real life doesn't always make sense. So to be clear, this is what happened, as it actually really truly did happen, as told by God Himself, in His Own Words*.

* Having invented the Universe, and, later that week, Man (and by extension all of Man's inventions including language spoken and written), everything within the Universe is God's; however, for the purposes of copyright and income tax, I hereby assert this work to be mine in entirety. It may not be copied either in part or in full, except with express written consent of the publisher, and for the purposes of dissemination of the Truth.

Buck Reidy, Editor

CONTENTS

ACKNOWLEDGMENTS

I would like to thank Holy God, without Whom this book could never have come to pass. Special mention also to the ancient desert people who invented Him.

GENESIS

In the beginning, God created Heaven and Earth.

God existed Himself before this 'beginning', so it was not the *beginning* beginning, as such, merely the beginning of recorded history. It is unknown what God was up to before this, because He didn't keep a journal, but it may have involved God creating Himself.

An unofficial and unsanctioned good-but-not-great book tells us that:

> "…Earth was without form, and void; and darkness was upon the face of the deep. And the Spirit of God moved upon the face of the waters."

For centuries, scholars have puzzled over what this means. Some argue it's meant to be poetic – one scholar noted its clear allusion to unploughed fields, a lamb and a prize heifer-in-calf. Others claim that it hints at God's vanity, and that the Deity was always admiring Himself in His reflection on the water, but since it was dark at that point in time, no one takes such suggestions seriously. Whatever the reason, He did what He did, when He did. And He did it all at the beginning of the working man's week: Monday morning.

Having created Heaven and Earth, God would have been within His rights to take it easy, but He wasn't called God for nothing.

Let there be light, He said. And there was light.

Ah thanks be to Me, He said. I couldn't see a damn thing.

Now, God continued, as He looked about: Okay, the part where I can see things is called Day, for Doris, and where I can see nothing, I will henceforth call it Knight, for Michael.

He stood back and surveyed His handiwork.

There! He announced to no one in particular: I'm pooped, but not a bad day's work done, if I do say so myself.

And with that, God was off home to Heaven, where He lived all alone, with microwave meals and floating fluff for flooring and walls.

The next day, Tuesday, God got up late and lounged around on His comfy couch-clouds in Heaven all morning, pleased with Himself for all He had done on Monday. Eventually He came down to Earth (as we all must) and looking about Him, said: Let there be a firmament in the midst of the waters, and let it divide the waters from the waters.

And lo! Land burst up out of the water, parting the water.

Ooh, that was pretty neat, said God, looking at the way the water peeled back from the land. I must remember that trick.

Having started work late, night was already beginning to fall, so God took off home to Heaven. Once there, He felt a pang of self-doubt. The old Tuesday evening blues.

What on Earth am I doing? He wondered. *That* wasn't a decent day's work, considering I created an entire Universe yesterday. Okay, tomorrow I'm really going to step up my workrate.

So saying, the microwave binged and He retrieved His chicken szechuan in its plastic container and ate quickly, burning His tongue only once.

On Wednesday morning, God looked down on Earth as He ate His porridge. The land had once more fallen beneath the water, undoing all His Good Work from the day before. As He blew upon His porridge to cool it, He had an idea, and said: Let the waters under the Heaven be gathered together unto one place, and let the dry land appear.

And it was so, and it looked great, except the water kept flowing back over all the world, Earth still being completely level and spherical and water being subject to something called gravity, which never took a break, unlike God.

After a bit of experimenting, God found that by pinching land between His thumb and forefinger, and pushing in other parts with the heel of His palm, He could make the water gather in some places and stay away from others.

Et voilà, He said. Dryness, wetness… a touch wetter on the whole, but you can't have everything.

By now, it was time for a teabreak, so God went up to Heaven and looked down with pride on His work. Unfortunately, He had no one to share it with, but He was getting around to that.

During tea, He decided to call the dryness Land, and the wetness Sea.

This is good, He said, and the blue sea is lovely and sparkly. However, land is a bit dull. The blue and the brown work well together, for sure, but it needs something to really make it pop from a distance, more…

He looked down at his colour chart.

More green! He said. Yes, more green, that'd be lovely, some texture. Dammit, my masterpiece needs life!

With that, He commanded the Earth to bring forth grass, and herbs, and fruit trees.

And they will all live and die and self-propagate, He said, and it was so.

By the time God was finished crafting all the little pears and mandarins and bananas, He was exhausted.

Let's call it a day, chaps, shall we? said God to Himself.

And with that, God was off home to Heaven.

On Thursday, God got up early and said: Let there be lights in the firmament of the Heaven to divide day from night; and let these lights be for signs, and for seasons, and for days, and years.

And God made two great big lights in the sky: one to

rule the day, and a nightlight for His future creations when they might need to find their way out of hovels for an emergency pee or the like.

While God was carving the sun into a circle, bits of light dust scattered all across the sky. He only noticed afterwards, when it was getting dark. By then, He was tired, so He pretended to Himself that it was on purpose, and named them the stars.

When He got up to Heaven, the daylight was fading out, disappearing to the west, which was a new thing for Him (both the light and its fading effect). He sat in Heaven with a tikka masala on His lap and admired the effect of the gathering dusk on the curvature of Earth before drifting off to sleep.

On Friday morning, God was awakened by a searing light.

Holy Myself, My Eyes are burning! What in the name of Me is that? He asked Himself.

It's the sun, He answered. I-you created it.

So I did, He replied to Himself. Well, it's a fine bit of work, the sun, but you wouldn't want to have had a few social drinks taken after work on a Thursday evening.

He got up and made His porridge, basking in the glow of the dawn, and looking at the blue-green ball below. It was good, but God wanted great: He was a perfectionist.

Animals, He said, snapping His fingers. Let there be creatures in the water, and fowl above the Earth, flying, except in the case of landbirds such as the ostrich and domestic fowl.

And just like that, fish and birds! Just like that. Proof,

if needed, of the strength of a good breakfast, an early rise and a regimen of vigorous calisthenics.

Then He made every other living creature, up out of the water. And He was chuffed, and blessed them, saying: Be fruitful, dear little animalses, and multiply, and let fish fill the waters in the seas, and let fowl multiply on Earth.

Then God went for tea in Heaven, with His legs dangling over the edge of Heaven while He looked at Earth with His brilliant eyesight and His notebook of great ideas.

Flying things, check. Floaty-swimmy things, check. Whoops... Tsk-tsk! He chided Himself. Where are the walky-movey things on the land?

After tea, He came down to Earth and said: Let there be cattle, and creepy-crawlies, and bellysnakes, and lumpyhorses and monkeys and so forth: and it was so forth, because whatever God said happened.

After a long hard week of making the Universe, one couldn't begrudge God a rest on Saturday... Pah! What nonsense, God never rests!

On Saturday, God looked down upon Earth. At this stage, He was immensely proud of all He had achieved, but something was lacking.

I need validation, He said, some obsequious miserable wretches. Let me pick one of the animals and elevate them above their station, to almost-me-but-really-not-even-close, so that they might wonder at my greatness and make me feel great and worship me.

Lion bounded about majestically, his mane blowing in the light savannah breeze.

Something about the animal put the Almighty in mind of pride, and thus He searched elsewhere.

An eagle soared high above, grace and power in combination.

Too elegant, thought God, and looked on.

The blue whale, enormous, gliding through the deep sea, rose to the surface and blew a spurt of water a hundred feet in the air.

Not bad, thought God, but perhaps too humble.

A hairy monkey grinned on a tree, as it poked about his nether regions with a stick and sniffed the results.

Perfect, said God.

He took one, straightened him up and shaved him bare, so he looked ridiculous, then boosted his mental faculty *just* a shade.

Now, said God, you I call Man.

Man shivered and grinned.

For a brief moment, God paused and reflected on what he was about to do.

I might regret this one day, He said.

And so say all of us, said Lion sullenly.

Quiet you, said God. You would have been chosen but for your pride.

What pride? said Lion. We lions are very modest creatures. Pride is just the collective term for us.

Right, said God, mentally chiding himself for forgetting this. Yeah well, no one likes pious humility either.

Lion growled and leapt beautifully away across the grass.

Now, said God, where is Man, that I might give him instruction on my worship?

He looked about and discovered Man, perched on a tree branch and poking his stick into a beehive.

You there, thundered God. What are you doing?

Nothing, sir, said Man, throwing the stick away and standing to attention on the branch. Due to a combination of fear and terrible balance, he fell from the tree and picked himself gingerly off the dusty ground.

Now, said God, I have some instructions for you. Be fruitful, and multiply, and replenish the Earth, and subdue it, and have dominion over the fish of the sea, and over the fowl of the air, and over every living thing that moveth upon the Earth.

Okay, said Man.

Did you get all that, said God.

Every word of it, sir.

Good. Repeat it back to me.

Em… be full of fruit… Multiply the fish and… em, something about subduing them, too?

God sighed wearily. It had been a long day, and a tough week.

Fine, He said. Good Man yourself.

Man beamed with pride. Lion raised an eyebrow and looked at God. God ignored him: he might not be proud, Lion, but he could still be one smug bastard.

On Sunday, God woke because of the searing light of the sun, but couldn't muster the energy to get out of bed, and merely pulled a fluffy cloud across to bring the darkness back.

Taking a close look at Earth early on Monday

morning, God noticed that the newly-created world was in danger of falling into complete chaos, on account of Man's idiocy.

One day, just *one* day? said God despairingly.

You're the one who put him in charge, noted Lion.

Shut up, Lion, said God, I wasn't asking you. Anyway, I'm fixing it.

And He was, too. God built a 'garden' with high walls and angels standing guard outside with flaming swords, and put Man in this garden, to let him think about what he had done for a while.

That's a prison, God, said Lion.

Don't you ever get sick of being right, you sanctimonious overgrown pussycat? said God.

The prison-garden of Eden was built to Victorian reform-of-prisoner ideals, as follows:

It was four-sided, with angels stationed in turrets at each of the corners. Each of the four walls was seven hundred metres long, thirteen metres high, and of solid drystone construction. The thickness of the walls at the base was two metres, and one at the top. Each of the angels took turns walking around the top of the wall and trimming back ivy and briars from the top of the wall, which might have aided the prisoner in an attempted escape. There was a gate, the sole entry and exit point, midway along the western wall.

Within the walls was a garden, with all manner of plants and trees. This was to calm and educate the prisoner, so that when ready to return to the world he would have a profession and abilities, and hobbies involving marigolds and geraniums.

A river passed through Eden, to water the plants, although regular rainfall or mist were both considered.

Now, Man, said God, this is your new home.

God brought Man to the Western gate and led him in.

Your home, Man, see? A big house all to yourself.

It has no roof, observed Man.

Have you been talking to Lion? asked God suspiciously.

Man looked confused.

Never mind, said God. You don't need a roof, Man. Now, you can eat anything in here, anything you like...

Great, said Man, reaching for the nearest fruit.

A sharp thwack across his knuckles had him howling in pain.

Except that tree. Nothing from that tree.

Then why's it here? asked Man.

Meh... temptation, plot device, tragedy – take your pick.

Upon this command, once more Man reached for the fruit.

Once more, God rapped his knuckles, and Man howled in hurt.

But you said– began Man.

Not from the tree, idiot; I meant *take your pick* from the list of reasons I gave you. Don't you listen to anything I say?

Yes, sniffed Man, I just don't understand you.

At this, God felt sympathy for the poor fool. He also realised that He had neglected to provide Man with a counterpart with whom he could carry out the multiplication part of His divine instructions.

Right, well, never mind all that now, said God soothingly. Have some berries and a little snooze here in the afternoon sun, there's a good little fellow.

Before long, Man was out cold. The narcoleptic berries were a wonderful invention, God thought, even if He did say so Himself.

He slapped some distilled berryjuice on a napkin and laid it over Man's snoring orifice and got to work.

With a deft Hand, he opened Adam's side up, cracked a rib out and resealed him, then crafted a female from the rib, and called this new creation Woman. Having had experience with Man, He made a much better job of Woman, and He was pleased. He laid her beside the sleeping Man and went back to Heaven for a microwave meal before bedtime.

When Man awoke, he had a searing pain in his side. He looked down to discover that he had a nametag pinned to his bare chest. Adam, he was called.

Ow, yelled Adam.

The sound of his voice awoke the woman. Eve, she was called, if her nametag was anything to go by.

Eve yelped with fright when she saw Adam. Adam screamed when he saw Eve, then looked about for a stick to kill her with: he hadn't progressed very far along the evolutionary tree as yet, but recognised in this other Man an improved version of himself. Thankfully, Adam lacked a stick with which to kill his rival, so he was unable to end the human race before it really got going (much to Lion's disappointment).

Subsequently, Eve employed a charm offensive to subdue the brute in front of her, and before long, Adam and Eve were inseparable.

CAIN AND ABEL

When a man loves a woman in a certain way, babies appear. Adam loved Eve in this manner, and Eve gave birth to a boy. They called him Cain.

Adam loved Eve in that special way again, though not for a while after Cain was born, because Cain was all little and cute and demanding of attention, but in the fullness of time, Adam got his chance, with candles and rose petals strewn about, and lo: Abel was born.

Having planned their future careers carefully – in the days before financial services and other lucrative industries, like dentistry, such options were limited – Cain became a tillage farmer, while Abel was a shepherd.

Cain was fine at his job, but Abel really excelled at being a shepherd. More than a shepherd, actually: an all-rounder, vertically integrating all aspects of his business, everything from animal husbandry and selective breeding to manufacture of various dairy products, lamb chops, other choice meat cuts, leather, glue by-products, not to mention selling the animal's slurry to his brother, so that

Cain could fertilise his crops. Abel was the first human to feature on the cover of *Time* magazine, as well as *Fortune's Top 50 Under 50*.

Cain looked on enviously at his brother's success but said nothing. When harvest time came around, Cain offered up to the Lord a selection of fruits and vegetables.

Oh, said God. Well. Thanks, Cain.

Cain was surprised by God's cool reaction, but figured He must be awkward about accepting gifts. Just as he was leaving God's presence, Cain saw Abel approaching in the distance, with a huge hamper, crammed full of the finest produce: steaks, hocks, hard cheeses, soft cheeses so strong they smelled of essence-of-toenail. There were leather gourds of champagne, leather belts, and handbags and wallets, even a signed copy of *Time*. Cain crept into a nearby bush, and overheard God say: Why, Abel, this is magn– No, this is too much, I couldn't– And the magazine, too!

Look, I signed it for you, right there.

Oh no, I couldn't.

Cain turned away in disgust and fury. God simpering over his brother was the final straw, in a lifetime of straws.

Enough, he vowed. This is sheepmuck, and I've had it up to here.

Later that evening, God came to Cain, and said: Cain, why the sad face?

Go away, God, said Cain huffily.

I can't *go away*, said God; I'm omnipresent.

Oh yeah, it's all about the presents with you, I can

see that.

Oh. Oh wait, is this about Abel's gifts?

You didn't even like mine.

Fruit and veg, Cain? Fruit and veg?! Come on, do I look vegetarian?

They're all I have to offer.

I said thank you.

Barely.

Now listen, said God, turning stern of a sudden: You're headed down a bad road, Cain. This is a destructive path, and I'd advise you to stop and think about what you want to achieve in life, you hear?

But Cain had already left, storming off towards his field.

God visited Abel on His way back up to Heaven, and asked him to talk to his brother. Abel of course acquiesced, and headed straight to Cain's field, where he was angrily pulling carrots up out of the ground.

Hey Cain, said Abel.

Fagawf, said Cain in a sullen tone.

I brought you something, Abel said, offering him a handmade genuine leather wallet.

I said, fagawf!

Are you angry with God, or with me? Because I haven't ever done you wrong, you know.

Cain whirled to face him, and Abel saw a carrot peeler in his hand.

Whoa, said Abel, backing away. Cain, have you been drinking the bad applejuice again?

You facking goody twoshoes. I'll show you.

So saying, Cain lumbered after Abel and swung the

peeler threateningly at his brother. In his drunken condition, however, he misjudged the peeler's arc, and sliced Abel's belly open.

Oh God, said Abel, as blood seeped forth from his stomach. Oh God, he repeated, then collapsed to the ground.

Feggit anyway, said Cain, and threw his carrot peeler away. Stumbling blindly through his tears and the undergrowth, he ran and hid beneath a bush.

Up in Heaven, God was crumpling the tinfoil carton from his microwave dinner into a ball and lining up a potshot for the trashcan when the doorbell rang.

That's odd, said God, pausing the tv. Who could that be?

He went to the pearly gates, and lo, there was Abel.

Abel, said God. I– I wasn't expecting you for about another eight hundred years or thereabouts.

I'm sorry, God, said Abel, I didn't expect to be here either.

Wow, it was… you know, I'd always thought Adam – your Daddy, I mean – would be the first up here. I had it in the notebook, see?

God went to his filing cabinet and opened the bottom drawer.

Dum-de-dum-dummm, He hummed as He flipped through the various folders, until He reached the one He wanted.

Aha, He said. He pulled out his spiral-bound notebook with *Earth* scrawled on the front and showed it to His unexpected guest.

Adam, nine hundred and thirty years old, cardiac

arrest, said God. Then next up is Eve, nine hundred and thirty five, complications arising from a botched manicure. Then it's Cain, then you, then Seth.

Who's Seth?

That's classified, but don't you worry about it. Sorry the place is in a mess, but as I say, I wasn't expecting anyone so soon. And my goodness, look at you, you're bleeding! Let's get that all fixed up and you can tell me what happened – was it a ram?

As God tended to Abel's wound, Heaven's newest occupant told Him what had happened.

God appeared before Cain, still huddled in the bush.

Cain, where is your brother?

I know not, said Cain insolently. Am I my brother's keeper?

No, you little bastard; you're his murderer!

Aargh, cried Cain, shrinking back from the big vengeful fellow. I'm sorry, it was an accident.

My eye, said God.

It was, honest to You. I was drunk and I only meant to scare him. Believe me, the hangover is punishment enough.

I'll be the Judge Judy and executioner of that, said God. From this day forward, you shall be a vagabond and a fugitive.

No! said Cain. That is too much for me. Everyone who finds me shall slay me.

This gave God pause for thought.

Notwithstanding, said the Creator, that you're currently one of only three people on Earth, and that you can only die once (unless you're my son or a

Buddhist), you have somewhat of a point. Therefore, I will make a mark upon you, so that others will think hard before causing you harm.

Completing his work on Cain (a tattoo on both cheeks saying *Protected by God*), God then spent some hours creating new men and women from stray grinning monkeys, appreciating the biological concerns associated with a horrendously narrow gene pool, especially one with such a murderous bent.

I thought my work here was at an end, God thought, what with creating the universe and a custodian for Earth, but I have a bad feeling it's only just beginning.

Now what? said Cain, as he inspected God's handiwork in a pool of water.

Now get out of my sight, you murderer, said God.

And with that, Cain was gone, headed east of Eden with a collection of seeds and pips to set up business thereabouts.

After a long week of travelling, he arrived at a small hamlet created from God's imagination and gene-splicing expertise.

Nod, read the sign, population 47.

Make that forty-eight, said Cain, throwing his bag of seeds on the floor of the local tavern, and hailing the publican: Have any cider and unmarried marriageable women, in that order?

Indeed we do, sir, said the publican, pouring him a frothy gourd of ApplePat's Strongbrew cider and a ticket for the next newly-created woman. Welcome to the land of Nod.

After two gulps of the brew, Cain was transported away to a sleepysleepy land of rest and recuperation, after which he woke to find himself married, with a kid called Enoch and living in a city he'd founded and named for his son.

Whoa, what happened? he said to himself, aloud.

You were out on the applesauce again last night, said his wife, Nameless.

Who're you?

I'm your wife.

What's your name?

Doesn't matter enough to be written down in the Bible, she said huffily. Anyway, there's a couple tonne of them parsnips to be dug up out of the earth this afternoon, or they'll rot in the ground.

And thus was Cain's life, all the days of his life, and for his wife Nameless, and their son Enoch, and all their descendents, though not for too many more generations, on account of the Flood, for therein was their family line extinguished and converted into mermaids and mermen, as retold in the fable Waterworld.

In the meantime, Adam and Eve were without child, to all intents and purposes. Adam wondered at their absence, and searched the fields and farm for signs of his two sons, but could find none. He returned to Eve and reported his failed expedition.

God, said Adam, shaking his head, God Almighty–

With that incantation, the Creator appeared before him.

–but what has become of the youth of today? finished Adam.

Ah, murdered and murderers, Adam, said God, but never mind, I will give you a new son.

What's wrong with the ones I have?

Had, you mean, corrected God. Abel's dead.

At this Adam sobbed. Eve came to the door to see who was there and what was going on.

Oh, it's You, she said to God.

Now now, said Adam, He's the reason we're alive.

He's the reason I had such pain giving birth, too, said Eve. I mean really, how could you—

Eve, enough! said Adam. Abel's dead.

I... I came to bring you good news, really, said God, thinking that in the future he might use messengers for delivering news, as this situation was turning awkward fast.

Oh, that our son is dead? That's fantastic, God, I suppose the other one's dead too?

Not as such, but Cain did kill Abel, so I had to banish him forever.

You... you banished him?! Oh *beau-ti-ful!* You are a piece of work, God. You really are something, you know that, you—

God fled the scene of the angry woman shouting and the grown man sobbing, and scooted off to Heaven in a cold sweat.

There, Abel was frying up lamb chops for dinner.

Ah, thought God, this sure beats a microwave dinner.

So saying, He tucked into his food and forgot all about the misery below on Earth.

Now, he said to Abel, how would you like a pair of wings?

Back on Earth, Eve gave birth to a new boy.

She sighed with relief, then began to cry.

Why are you crying? said Adam to Eve, as he too began to cry.

I was hoping for a girl, said Eve. How about you?

Empathy, said Adam, dabbing away his tears. Let's call this one Seth.

And Seth was Adam & Eve's son's name from that day forward, although he didn't have a birth certificate so the state declared him a non-person and refused to issue him a passport. For that reason, he stayed close to home, consolidating the vegetable and meat industry begun by his two brothers who were never again mentioned.

In time, Seth got with one of the more recently-created women, to give Adam and Eve grandchildren, and to continue the family business after he passed (d. 912 yrs). His son, Enos (d. 905 yrs) passed the business onto Cainan (d. 910 yrs), who passed it to Mahaleel (d. 895 yrs), who passed it to Jared (d. 962 yrs), who passed it to Enoch (d. 365 yrs, tragically and too soon, in an accident involving an early prototype of the wheel, a thirteen tonne semi-rounded stone that he and others had carried to the top of a hill in order to demonstrate the benefits of its use – the wheel was outlawed shortly after Enoch was buried (or more accurately, left to rot under the prototype)). Methuselah (d. 969 yrs), left in charge of the business after his father's untimely death, let it go to ruin, before passing what was left of the food and manufacturing conglomerate to Lamech (d. 777 yrs). Lamech was a lazy scoundrel and blew the remains of the business on speculative investments that went sour, leaving his son, Noah, with a need for a day job.

NOAH

By now, the world human population had grown exponentially.

Those monkeys, said Lion distastefully. It's a disgrace, the way they breed. You'll regret the day you created them, I'm telling you.

They're not monkeys now; they're humans, said God, and besides, you're just jealous.

Well, you'll see, said Lion, and with a mighty roar, he bounded across the plain in search of a breeze that would make his mane blow in a more elegant fashion.

Lion had observed, quite correctly, that the people were breeding like rabbits, and furthermore, they were beginning to act the goat.

One day God looked down and saw that a group of the humans had written something on the ground using white stones. Unfortunately the ground itself was fairly white, being in the desert and all that, so God had to have a closer look.

He zoomed in on the world, squinting to see the

writing against the brightness of the sun on the desert sand, and saw that they had written: *If you're squinting to see this, you're an idiot.*

He realised that the accursed humans were laughing at him.

Bastards, He said: Right, I'll show them.

God created an angel, and named him Ricky, and sent him down to do His bidding, including clearing the white stones. When a month of celestial time had passed and Ricky had not returned, God once more cast His gaze upon Earth to look for His angel.

God found Ricky. Ricky did not find God. Ricky was flaming. Not in a homosexual sense, nor in a culinary manner, although, to be sure, Ricky was also cooked. He was inebriated, sauced, ossified, blathered, smashed and stupefied. He was furthermore wasted, hammered, and bananas.

Ricky! came forth a Voice from the clouds.

Gad, gad, gadgadgaddygad, replied God's messenger on Earth.

Ricky, what are you doing?

Ha! said Ricky, then hiccupped.

Ricky, what are you doing? Have you done my bidding?

What?

Have. You. Done. My. Bidding?

A long pause coupled with much lolling of Ricky's head from side to side was followed with: What?!

Then God looked to Ricky's side. There was an empty gourd of wine.

Bastards, said God once more. Right.

With a celestial swoosh, a bolt of lightning struck Ricky and he lost his wings, condemned to be a man for the rest of his shortened life.

Needless to say, God was more than a shade annoyed, and decided to hold a conclave in Heaven to decide what to do.

If God was truly searchingly honest with Himself, He had kind of let Earth run a little astray while concentrating on defeating the level-baddy on another world that was getting very complex: Magic Kingdom, it was called, or something.

Ahem, said God. I call this meeting to order.

There was silence. Adam examined his fingernails.

Well, Addy? said God.

Please, God, I hate Addy. Call me Adam.

Okay, Adam, said God. You people are really pissing me off. You're all messing around, killing one another, running around lawless, not taking any care of the animals, and now you've gone and messed up Ricky Angel…

I know.

I'm tempted to kill off the human race.

Please, no, Lord, said Adam.

Well then, what do you suggest?

What about ritual cleansing?

You mean, like…?

I dunno, a bath or something.

God had, has, and always will have, a wicked sense of humour. He allowed himself a little chuckle and said to Adam: Hmmm, a bath. Very good, Addy. Thank you, back you go into the VIP lounge.

Adam wasn't a fan of the 'VIP lounge' – in reality, a

23

secure area in Heaven not so different to Eden – or of being called Addy, but as God explained, you couldn't expect to live forever without a few minor inconveniences. The truth was, apart from Abel, God didn't trust Man not to mess up Heaven, too.

Now, then, said God, displaying His command of language and all things present, past and future using only seven letters and a comma.

He looked down on Earth and espied Noah. Noah was a park ranger for the Dead Sea Memorial Park, and perhaps the best-behaved of the humans.

The Dead Sea Memorial Park commemorated the death of the body of water known as the Aabee Sea, nominally named for Abraham, the father of all people (except the Red Indians and the Chinese and the Africans. Also except the Mongolians, Pacific Islanders, Native South Americans and Aboriginal Peoples of Australasia. Possibly also excluding the Russians, homo erectus and penguinians, although genetic studies are inconclusive in these respects).

Abraham hadn't yet been born, but no one was certain about this: what they *were* certain about was that Abraham was not living, therefore he was dead, in their estimation, and so was the sea commemorating him. Originally, the Aabee Sea had been renamed the Dead Aabee Sea, but as so often happens, the middle bit got lost through linguistic shorthandery and laziness, and it was now known simply as the Dead Sea.

Noah was probably the only good guy left on Earth, born of humble stock but noble lineage, going all the way back to Adam. He rarely took baksheesh for allowing tourists to float on the water, unlike the other rangers. He didn't force camels to drink the water, which was poisonous for the poor lumpyhorses. He had no more than a moderate amount of mistresses secreted about the sea perimeter, and all his manchildren were reasonably good folk, albeit a little lazy in his eyes.

Right, said God. (He said such words a lot, as He didn't have anyone to talk to, and thus tended to punctuate His thoughts with expositions of sound whenever the thoughts threatened to lead to action.)

Still smarting from the farce that was the expedition of Ricky Angel, God took matters into His own Hands, and went down to meet with Noah, disguised as a crafty tourist, a shapeshifting trick He had picked up from his mate Zeus.

Noah, said God.

Feck off, tourist, said Noah.

He wasn't in the form for rejecting bribes, having been stymied in his advances towards his favourite mistress last night.

Get away from me, you ancient fecker, she had said.

She was correct. Noah was eight hundred years old, and had the physique to prove it.

Noah, said God, if you give that lumpyhorse a bucket of the seawater, I'll give you the body of a four-hundred-year-old.

Tourist, clear off now and leave the camels alone.

Satisfied that Noah was an upstanding man, God revealed Himself.

Holy God, that's an almighty one, exclaimed Noah.

Now you know who I am, listen to me, said God. I'm going to rain down vengeance on this world because it's gone rotten. However, I'm not giving up on the human race completely, so I'm letting you live, because you're a good guy.

Thanks God, said Noah.

Hold on, said God. First, I want you to build a boat—

No problem.

—big enough for you and your sons—

Them layabouts? Fair enough.

—and their wives—

Oh Christmas, thought Noah, but he just said: Fine.

—and two of every animal in the world, male and female—

Hmmm, said Noah.

—and your wife, said God in conclusion.

Ah here look, God, said Noah, I'd rather take my chances at drowning, to be honest.

Well, you've no choice in the matter, you ungrateful little shit, said God.

Fine, said Noah grumpily. Anything else?

Yes. All the plants of the world and enough food for everyone.

Sweet mother. Food for how long?

I don't know yet.

Right, said Noah, what do I get in return?

What?

In return.

You inherit the Earth.

Sure I've enough to be minding as it is. I don't want any more.

Your children will inherit the Earth.

Let them go and fuck, the lazy articles.

Noah... said God in a tone that brooked no argument.

Yes, God? replied the human warily.

Just do it, right?

Noah sighed and relented. Fine, God, said Noah, there's just one thing...

What is it, Noah?

Can I bring one mistress?

Sherazdna'a?

Yeah.

Fair enough, but if anyone–

I'll keep her in with the camels, and let no one but myself feed them.

I don't want anyone else to hear of this, Noah. No boasting.

Sure I've no one to boast to, God, all my friends will be gone, only them useless sons of mine. I tell them nothing.

But Noah was only speaking to the wind, as God had disappeared back to Heaven.

Noah set to doing his calculations for the size of the boat and brought them to Schillman and Sons, Dead Sea Yachtmakers.

That's a pretty big yacht, said Schillman Sr, sucking in through his teeth. It'll set you back a pretty penny. Do you want it made of stone, wood or bronze?

What's bronze?

A thing we're making from burning bits of stone.

Like terrazzo?

No, not like that.

Carbon-fibre?

Hmm, heavier and shinier.

Look, said Noah. What's cheapest?

Wood.

How much?

Pre-currency prices notwithstanding, the figure Schillman Sr quoted him nearly knocked Noah down.

I don't have that kind of pre-currency-barter-unit lying around, said Noah.

Not many would, said Schillman. Of course, if you want to build it yourself... he laughed.

Screw you, Schillman, said Noah, that's exactly what I'll do.

Schillman fixed him with a stern gaze. That's against guild rules, Noah. No one builds boats around here without being a guild member.

It's not a boat, Schillman, it's just a giant wooden box.

Ho-ho, said Patrick O'Flaherty, union representative, undertaker and carpenter. Carpentry is it? You'll be wanting one of us from the Timberbuilders Union then, me ladeen. By law.

The hell I will, said Noah. You can all sod off. It's a family DIY project, and no one else is invited.

With that, he fled from the boatyard and general guild-and-trade-union assembly area to his homestead.

God help me, he said, where will I get the timber for this?

It was a valid question. The Dead Sea and its surrounds were largely bereft of foliage larger than a low shrub, mostly on account of the goats and sheep, but also owing to the dry climate.

That'll change soon enough too, thought Noah, but I don't have time to wait around.

He sent a letter to God via Santa Claus, to clarify how much time he had before the flood.

Just enough, came back the curt response.

Typical politician's answer, said Noah to himself. Right, well, I'll have to either get the timber myself or steal a boat big enough.

Neither option was particularly good, as Noah wasn't powerful enough to get away with thievery nor was he wealthy enough to buy the raw material, but if there's one thing he was, it was determined. And a problem-solver. And a prude (more on that later). In fact, there was no one thing that defined Noah. He was a jack of all trades, but right now it was his problem-solving abilities that were to the fore.

Talking to a man he knew who knew things from reading scrolls, Noah determined that wood could be found in the west.

Heading west, Noah entered the woods of Anatolia, and there came upon a clearing. Enlisting the aid of a number of swarthy types – in return for some Eastern spices and the promise of the secret to making Dead Sea Delights, a jellied confection – Noah managed to draw out ten thousand great trees and gather them on a plateau towards the north of Syria.

Not long after, a sign was erected just to the south of this plateau proclaiming:

> *Unclaimed Land: Guilds and Union rules do not apply beyond this point.*

Noah had made this sign himself, as an experiment in timber technology, and felt more at ease about tackling the big boat project with a previous one under his belt.

Having laid out all the trees, notching them and carefully marking out which segments would connect to which, Noah once more sent a letter to God via Santa Claus, to clarify how much time he had before the flood.

Just enough, came the reply.

Right, said Noah, in perfect imitation of God. He set to work and sent for his wife and sons and daughters-in-law, but not until a month after he had sent for Sherazdna'a.

That was a happy month for him, banging and nailing and hammering all day long. Still, all good things come to an end.

The all-rolling canoe – or ARC – neared completion when one day Noah espied in the distance a great caravan of people approaching.

Quick, Sherazdna'a, he said. Into the camel room with you.

They had discussed their plan long in advance of this day, and so Sherazdna'a made for the compartment she was to share with the camels.

A quick closing up of the secret hidey-hole with some stale bagels thrown in for good measure, and Noah was ready to face the throng.

What in the hell are you doing, you old goat? said his wife in warm greeting.

Darling, replied Noah. How lovely to see you. And legitimate children, do come in.

Everyone entered the ark and began staking out their rooms and discussing their plans to knock through into adjoining rooms until Noah halted them with a shout.

Hey!

They turned to look at him as he continued: Now listen. No one is knocking through any walls after I went to all the trouble of building this bloody thing. Every bit of timber in this ARC is structurally required. Built by me, but designed by iGod in California.

What's California? asked Shem, one of Noah's sons.

Noah punched him in the mouth.

That is, he said. Anyone else have any questions?

Seeing that Noah was in one of *those* moods, the crowd grew silent.

Very good. Now, everybody is to go out and collect two of every creature you espy. Land, sea or air, bring them to me. Well, okay, not sea, they'll be fending for themselves.

Thus saying, he sent Shem north, with responsibility for creatures beginning with letters A to F. Hem was sent east, for creatures from G to N. Japheth went west for those from O to Y, and Noah headed south for the rest, including the magnificent Zebra.

What shall we do? said the womenfolk.

Gather up some hay and make soup and latkes. We're going on a family vacation when I get back, he said.

Then Noah headed down to the savannahs and returned astride a male zebra, leading the female behind on a length of rope.

Leaping off the barcoded pony, Noah herded the

two animals down to the end of the ARC, third level, then went in search of his checklist that God had sent.

Walking along the deck, ticking off the animals, Noah noticed the letter U was missing.

Wait, where are them goathorse things? he cried. Looking at his ledger, he cross-checked the name once more.

The… the unicorns, who had charge of them?

Shem and Hem instantly pointed to Jepheth.

Treacherous bastards, snarled Jepheth.

Enough, you oaf, roared Noah. I'm going down to see what else you fools have missed.

Noah came back two days later, having spent most of that time in the camel stabling, but a little of it in counting up the missing creatures.

There are no dragons, he announced. All the animals beginning with X are missing, he said, glaring at Japheth. The baggerballs are not in their cage, the Alpine biped-jelly-creature is nowhere to be seen and we have not one marmaduke. Not one. You have disappointed me greatly, sons.

The sons paid him no attention. He was over eight hundred years old and his voice was as dry as the scratches of a pen on parchment.

What do you all say to this?

Again they ignored him.

Pah! he said and shook his fist at them. Storming out of the ARC sub-penthouse suite, he sent a letter to God.

Ready when you are.

Good. I hope you double-tarred it, said God's response.

Oh flip, I forgot the tarring, said Noah.

Whoosh, came the reply from God, as a deluge of water emptied from above onto Earth.

Wheeee and Glug-glug-glug, said the ARC, as it took off on the flood and took on board a large volume of water.

Noah sent his sons below to keep bilging the coffers, within which many animals were quartered. The absence of pitch and subsequent semi-drowning of many creatures – the long-snouted blue pig, obesehorse, elephantus maximus and some strain of the gigantic legless Friesian bovines amongst them – led to the development of sea mammals (the seal, walrus, dolphin and killer whale being commonly-known examples).

Lazy articles, said Noah. Now, I must tend to the camels.

Again? exclaimed his wife. Can't someone else do it?

Don't get between a man and his camels, said Noah and stormed out of the penthouse suite.

Forty days and forty nights of rain, then one hundred and fifty days and nights more. It was enough to drive a man mad, which was exactly where Noah was headed. He had neglected to renew his Netflix subscription too, so there was nothing on the television except reruns of Desperate Housewives Season Four and the static from the beginning of the universe on the other channel.

Day one-ninety-one of the incessant misery and wetness came to a close, and Noah went for his evening's entertainment.

Thank God for Sherazdna'a, he thought, as he clambered in amongst the camels and waded through their shit to the secret hidey-hole.

Thanks for nothing, God, thought Noah, as he clambered out of the secret hidey hole.

Sherazdna'a had perished from the stink of the camels.

Poor me, said Noah. It has stopped raining but the bathtub of the world is still plugged.

God had forgotten about him, Noah was certain. He opened a porthole and sent a dove with a letter to Santa Claus to this effect. The dove did not return, which Noah took as either a good or a bad sign. He didn't mind the loss of the dove: the damn things were multiplying faster than the rats, and only for the two species mutually preying on one another, the ship would certainly have been overrun with either one.

His repeated entreaties to God via Santa Claus were in vain, as the Laplandish sweatshops and factory outlets had been covered in the deluge, and the furtive fat festive fellow had perished, though he would be born again, like all good men.

God, meanwhile, was in fact busy with a particularly tasty conundrum in another world in another universe, and it was only in passing on his way to a toilet break that he noticed that Earth was still entirely blue.

Well that's not right, said God, and set a wind to blow the water down from the high parts to the low parts.

Once more Noah sent two doves and a raven out of the ark, as well as thirty rats and twenty snakes, though that was just to watch the bastards drown.

One returned. Of the doves, that is, with an olive branch.

Where in God's name did you get that? asked Noah.

On the dry land to the east of here, replied the dove.

You can speak? replied Noah, astonished.

No, but the fumes you are ingesting from the stables have a similar effect to LSD, replied the dove, then turned into a winged hippopotamus and fluttered away towards the sun before exploding into a rainbow.

Christ, said Noah, presciently, then opened the door of the ark and stepped out onto dry land.

Simultaneously, his wife burst open one of the windows and said: Thanks be to God, a bit of sunshine.

Two minutes later, she had bustled through the back hatch and erected a clothes line, onto which an assortment of rags and cloths were rapidly being attached.

The first bit of drying we've had all summer, she exclaimed to Noah, who was busy corralling one of each species into a fenced-off area. He then proceeded to douse them in petrol.

He had just cast a match onto this mass of living creatures when God landed down from Heaven.

Hey Noah, what smells good...?

Then seeing where the smell was coming from, God used his Superman breath to quench the flames on the blackened carcasses.

What the opposite-of-Heaven did you do that for? said God.

I was sacrificing in your honour... said Noah.

With one out of the only two creatures of each species?

I just thought–

You just *thought*?! said God. Well, I wish you *would*,

Noah, I wish you would. How can these species propagate now that you've killed off the male or female of each one.

Suitably chastened by this telling-off, but still in a huff over the loss of Sherazdna'a, Noah muttered to himself: Well, it would've been easier if you'd made them asexually reproductive.

What did you say? cried God, turning angry and vengeful.

Nothing God, I was only sacrificing them for you, said Noah sullenly.

Hmmph, said God. Alright then. Ctrl + Z.

With that magic phrase, the sacrificed beasts were brought back to life.

Ah, thanks God, said Noah, brightening up.

Fine, said God. Next time you're making an offering, just go with some patchouli incense sticks or something.

I won't be so foolish again, said Noah.

And he wasn't. In fact, for the most part, Noah was a very sensible man until the end of his days (apart from the nakedness, as we shall see). The same could not be said for his offspring, however, who time and time again thoughtlessly extinctified another species until the only one left was Man. But that's jumping way ahead in the great Biblical story, when there's so much more left yet to tell.

The animals ran free, or slithered or crept, depending on their ambulatory skills. Special mention here of the pigs, who hithertofore were the most fastidiously clean of all God's creatures. Unfortunately, they were put in a lower level of the ARC that was reserved for earthworms and other creatures of the earth by Japheth, so that when they emerged after the flood had abated, they had grown accustomed to being in the muck and dirt.

While all the animals frolicked about, their god (God) and master (Noah) looked upon them and discoursed.

So Noah, all of these things you see, the plants and the animals, of these you may eat.

Thanks, God, but I'm stuffed after the lamb, to be honest.

No, not today, for all time.

Oh right. Yes, indeed. Well, that's great, and thanks again.

Hold it, I'm not done—

I bloody knew it, thought Noah. I knew there'd be more.

—it's only fair that they shall now fear you, so they are more difficult to catch and kill, but... but if they attack you, you may get your revenge, but they can't get you back, because you're my favourite.

Noah smiled at this.

Lion, listening from a nearby bush, growled under his breath, and skulked away, far from the habitation of Man.

And thereafter, God left Noah to multiply once more upon the face of the Earth, though with predispositions to certain defects on account of God's obliteration of the gene pool necessary for a truly healthy species.

In celebration of escaping the ARC, Noah grew vines and harvested the grapes. One night, having drank the fermented juice, he became intoxicated and fell about his tent in the nip before knocking himself out cold.

Canaan, his son, chanced to enter the tent, looking for some wine. Upon discovering his father, he withdrew in convulsions of laughter. His other sons, divining what had happened, walked in backwards – or so they claimed – and covered Noah in a blanket.

For some unknown reason, Noah was very particular that none of his boys should see him naked. He had a complex, perhaps, about his tiny aged male genitals. In any case, when he awoke covered in a blanket that did not belong to him, he intuited that his sons must have seen him naked.

He thereupon called a meeting of the four boys in his tent.

What's this about, then? said Jepheth.

Who came in here, said Noah, while I was in the nip?

Hem, said Canaan, clearing his throat.

I did not, said Hem.

Once more, Noah regretted his choice of name for the boy.

Shem? asked Noah.

Nope, wasn't me, Pops.

Noah knew then that it was Canaan.

Canaan, my dear son, he said, with a clout in the face for emphasis: It was you, wasn't it?

It wasn't, sir, said Canaan.

You lying little bollix, said his father.

At the mention of small parts, Canaan giggled

despite himself, and Noah knew he *had* seen him naked.

Right, that's it, said Noah to Canaan. You're indentured for eternity.

Ah come on, Dad, that's not fair, said Japheth, Shem and Hem in unison.

That means he's your slave for life, said Noah to them.

At this, they demurred from their previous hasty response, insisting that it was reasonable enough punishment for seeing the old man in a state of undress. They divided Canaan on a roster, with Jepheth getting him on Mondays and Thursdays, Shem on Tuesdays and Fridays, and Hem on Wednesdays and Saturdays.

Who gets him on Sunday? they wondered aloud.

Day of rest, Canaan said. I'm demanding it off, pending an outcome on the claim I'm bringing against the imposition of slavery on me in the first place. *And* I'm putting in for a week off in summer.

Since God had Himself made the rule about one day of relaxation, Shem, Hem and Jepheth let it stand for now, but vowed amongst themselves to lobby for more liberal working conditions in the future.

Thereafter, the sons and daughters of Noah and his sons spread forth and were plentiful and lived in peace and harmony, until a big construction project occurred at a place called Babel.

THE TOWER OF BABEL

It came to pass that there was a large plain, where all of mankind lived together in perfect harmony.

A modern equivalent would be New York City, with Italians, Irish, Jews, Ethiopians, Chinese, Nigerians, Japanese, Slavs, British, and all the other races of man (apart from those exterminated, like the original men of the Americas and Australia.)

But Babel was different. Here in Babel, everyone got along great. Everyone spoke the same language. And in the spirit of brotherly love, they decided to build some sort of monument to show how well they were getting along and how much everyone liked everyone else. Truly, this was Heaven on Earth.

So they sent out an invitation to tender for the design and construction of this new monument. All manner of bizarre entries came back, because, well, architects. Say no more.

One entry outlined the construction of a great monolith-like edifice, that was in fact made up of stones gathered by every living person. And that was a lovely touch, but well, it was still just a big rock at the end of it all, and there was no shortage of those in the desert. Another entry called for a whole new city of marble; still another to level the narrow streets of Babel and replace them with boulevards, but as no one yet knew what a boulevard was, Hausmann had to bide his time with that particular scheme. No one really came up with anything that was truly different, until the judges came across the clear winner.

Aha, they said to one another, passing the scroll with the plans along to the next fellow, nodding and prodding the parchment with their forefingers.

Now *this*, they said, *this*.

Indeed, this.

What had been proposed was a *tower*. Something vertical, incredibly tall, and not squat and massive, but rather elegant, slender and impossibly high. They had to invent all sorts of new words to describe it, because it was like nothing they had ever seen before.

It's wonderful, they said. This man wins, this guy Askarpar, and now let's get to building this monument.

Of course, with all the new lingo, *this guy Askarpar* became a garbled term for the new building type.

Some Biblical historians point to Man's hubris in building the tower as the reason for the destruction of Babel, and they are correct, but not in the way they think.

To start with, Askarpar hadn't meant to invent a new building type; in fact, he hadn't even meant to enter the competition, but had mislabelled the address he was

41

sending his drawing to. He had also mislabelled the vertical and horizontal axes, so that what should have been a long low one-storey building on the outskirts of town became a massive tower right in the middle. In short, he was sloppy, was old Askarpar, which didn't bode well for a new form of construction.

What do you call this support? a builder would ask him.

And what about *this* one? another would ask.

Askarpar had to make names up on the spot. Not being very inventive, and with his relatively vertical Hiberno-Indian sons close to hand, he named the tall things for them.

Colm and Pilar, he said.

And so it went. Before long, terms such as spirit levels, overtime, retaining walls, and extras became widely known amongst those involved on the construction project. Those not involved began to perceive a linguistic rift developing, but were powerless to do anything.

No one stopped to question Askarpar's plan, imagining that it must have been divinely sent. Askarpar himself, however, was seriously troubled. He could barely design mud-brick houses, yet found himself in charge of the biggest edifice that had ever been built. To stave off a mental breakdown, he resorted to drinking and delegation, employing only those who wouldn't question his authority.

His delegates were unsure of how to proceed, as there simply *was* no precedent. The building was already twelve houses high, bigger by eleven than anything that had ever been built before. One brave underling brought this to his attention.

Higher, higher! screamed Askarpar, then threw the only set of drawings into the fire in a mock-rage.

There, he said to himself, no one can ever claim this thing was my idea now.

Back on site, the delegates were having grave doubts about Askarpar's abilities, and began to develop the structure autonomously.

This bit here, you see, said one to another: See how it doth crumble, and this other part, sinks into the mud?

Hmm, said the other, should we tell him?

He knows aught about it, said the first, let us thicken the base and shore up the foundations, then tell him we cannot build it any further.

We cannot go higher, they reported to Askarpar.

He struck them with a rod, cursed them and demanded that they double the height of the building and add gargoyles on the corners, transfer beams at the third floor and install a swimming pool and a library on the penthouse level.

What's a penthouse? they wondered.

Is it like a pentateuch? asked one.

You figure it out, he screamed and retired to his offices.

All the signs pointed in the direction of disaster, but despite the odds stacked against them, the delegates made a beautiful job of it. The building stood up, and everyone in Babel was happy.

Now, what do we do with it? they wondered.

We put the apartments on the market, the estate

agents confidently asserted: They'll sell like the proverbial hot-latkes.

What the hell's a proverb? asked one.

We're not there yet, said another.

The tower project began to disintegrate the fabric of society, driving wedges between all God's people, but the tensions were clearly not God-related; rather, they were the result of a number of factors related to the construction of the tower.

Firstly, the budget had been blown, leading to the invention of tax, and much grumbling of the populace. Further, and crucially, the building blocked natural light from many of the homes to the east and west of it, angering those who lived there and setting up disharmony between the East and West dwellers and the North and South citizens, who implied that the East-Westies were simply overreacting.

The East and West refused to pay their tax, understandably, leading to the invention of a group of citizens tasked with enforcing the tax. These were the original police force, and they had broad accents and knew how to *wield a cudgel, begoddenden*, as they put it. In order to keep their activities against the East and West hidden, the police began to use many code-words, leading to misunderstandings and mistrust between them and the general public.

Similarly, the architects and their brethren were by now speaking unintelligibly, using phrases such as 'the essence of space reflects the timeless nature of the freedom of material to speak to us honestly' and 'space enclosed makes gods of mere men'.

No one knew what they were talking about, and they seemed suspicious, so the police force rounded them up and locked them away, assuming they were plotting to destroy the building.

Interior designers and estate agents had also developed dialects of their own, speaking of space and light, textures, single- and dual-aspect, downpayments, investments, fixtures & fittings, spacious accommodation and other new words to describe, in more glowing terms than the existing words, the mundane aspects of the tower.

The delegates, the ones who had actually managed the building's construction, were on the brink of madness, having dedicated themselves entirely to the building and nothing else for the past seven years. They spoke in gibberish that was only understood amongst themselves: schedules, workforce, labour units, incremental productivity increases, milestones and so on. The police rounded them up and threw them in a cell next to the architects.

The tax-dodging East-West dissenters had taken to meeting in secret in the darkness of the East and West to plot the overthrow of the police and the detonation of the building. Of course, in such uncertain times, it was necessary for them to speak code also: proletariat, pigs, bourgeoisie, capitalist overlords, revolution, dynamite and liberty were all coined by these weak pasty-faced individuals, lacking melatonin and vitamin D from the perpetual shade of the Tower of Babel.

The police rounded these dissenters up, but having no more cells in which to put them, installed them in the swimming pool of the tower. Fatally, they failed to search them first.

The dissenters could not believe their luck – their main topic of discussion for the past two weeks had revolved around how they might gain access to the Tower of Babel, which was now heavily guarded by the police force.

Pledging their undying loyalty (a short-lived thing indeed) to one another, they held hands, chanted Kum-bi-Yah, My Lord, and detonated their devices.

With a terrible din, the magnificent tower of Babel came tumbling to the ground, levelling great tracts of the city of Babel. In despair, the few survivors began to leave in groups mutually distrustful of each other, and blaming everyone but themselves, in their new dialects, for what had happened.

Priests and scribes subsequently tasked with writing histories were keen to blame the tower's destruction upon the hubris of man, and the vengeance of a vengeful God that they (and they alone) could commune with. The truth is, Man alone was to blame, through an inability to get along in the face of increasing complexity. Through a division of labour into constituent parts and overreaching, thus was mankind separated into its races of the modern world, paving the way for the economists to come along and explain everything.

Now, one of the men who fled the destroyed town was Noah's son Shem's great-great-great-great-great-great-grandson Terah, named for a chocolate orange in Yorkshire. This man Terah had three boys: Abram, Nahor, and Haran. Two of them came to nothing, and one came to inherit the Earth.

ABRAM AKA ABRAHAM

Having led a relatively sedate life up until his nuptials, Abram married Sarai. The Lord appeared unto Abram upon the eve of his honeymoon, and He said to him: Abram, get your wife and come with me.

What is it, God? said Abram, I've a camel-train booked for early tomorrow morning for the honeymoon and I still have these twenty-five sheep to milk this evening.

Change of plan, said God, incinerating the sheep with his finger.

You bastard, thought Abram, looking at his carbonised ex-ovine stock in dismay.

I still owed money on those sheep, he said to God.

All the more reason for you to hightail it out of Haran then, isn't it? said God. Come on, go get the missus. This property I'm going to show you won't stay on the market forever.

Wait, we have to leave Haran for good? But I love it here.

Look, said God, the new place is worth it, I promise you.

So Abram headed back to the tent to pack up his few worldly possessions.

Sarai was drying meat ahead of their road trip the following day, and was surprised to see him return so soon.

You're back early, Abram.

Pack your bags, Sarai, we're getting out of here.

What? When?

This second.

Wait, she said. What should I bring? Will be going out to dinner in fancy restaurants?

Just get the slavegirl, will you, and let's get going? Come on, don't keep Him waiting.

Him who? The man on the moon? Who are you talking about? asked Sarai.

God, said Abram.

Oh beautiful, thought Sarai, but she kept her counsel. Her mother had warned her about Abram, but she had paid no heed.

I'm telling you, her mother had said: That Abe, he's no good for you.

Oh Mummy, you're such a worrywart, Sarai had laughed.

She wasn't laughing now.

Abram and Sarai set off across the desert with their goods, and at length, arrived upon a hill high above a vast plain.

Now, just stay here a moment, said Abram, God said he wants to talk to me in private.

Likely story, said Sarai. You're lost as usual.

Quiet! he said, and went forward to the edge of the mountain to parlay with the Creator.

So, what do you think of the view, Abram? asked God.

Nice, said Abram, keeping well back from the edge.

In truth, the view was bleak, barren and dusty, but he didn't feel like saying that to God, who seemed to have a bit of a vicious streak.

Behold, Abram, said God, unto thy seed I give this land.

What seed?

Your descendents.

Oh, right... Wait, what? All of this land?

Yes.

Gee, thanks God.

See, I told you it was worth your while.

Wow, this is fantastic. What a wedding present, God. How do we get down there?

As he spoke, Abram edged to the precipice and began figuring out how to descend the cliff-face.

Wait, wait. Get back up here, Abram. It's not yours; it's your descendents, said God, figuring that with Abe's low sperm count, it was an easy promise to make and an easy one to keep, but it only takes one fly to ruin an ointment, as the old saying went, and Abe had a few swimmers tucked away to ruin God's divine plan.

Well, what'd he have to say for himself? asked Sarai

when Abram returned.

He said all this land will belong to my descendents, said Abram.

Did he indeed? said Sarai, with no small lack of belief. All zero of them. Well, that's big of him; how come I can't see him?

Oh, He doesn't appear much to women anymore, Abram replied.

Hmmph, likely story! said Sarai. So, are we going there now or what?

Well, actually, we're not going to settle there, only our descendents.

Jeez, this God takes some beating, said Sarai. Any more worthless promises from him?

But Abram said nothing, sinking into a sullen silence. He led the camel back the way they had come and turned at the I5 intersection signposted for Egypt and all other traffic.

The following morning, they headed out across the Sinai desert for Egypt. They were now man and wife, so Abram was on a high with thoughts of the lovemaking to come.

This honeymoon will be great, said Abram; let's pretend while we're in Egypt that you're my sister.

And that was the end of any funny business for the honeymoon. Sarai had expected the Maldives for a fortnight; instead, she was on a sweaty hike across the desert, sleeping rough by the side of the road and living on snails' eggs and scorpions.

I didn't know snails laid eggs, said Sarai one morning, as she gagged on her breakfast.

What the hell's a snail? asked Abe, as he blew out the campfire. Come on, if we don't get moving for shelter before the sun's up, we'll burn to death.

Upon arriving in Egypt, things took a turn for the better — financially, at least — as Pharaoh chanced upon Abram and his wife, and took a shine to the beautiful Sarai, becoming Abe's best bud upon being told that Abe was Sarai's brother, and not husband as one might reasonably have expected.

Here's some more worldly possession, my best friend, said Pharaoh, bestowing further camels and gold jewellery upon Abe: Is your sister coming out with us tonight?

No, I don't think so, said Abram glumly, caught in the lie he'd only invented to add some roleplay spice to the honeymoon sex that he wasn't having on account of the spice.

Eventually, Abe could stand the deceit no longer. He came clean to Pharaoh.

What?! said Pharaoh. She's your wife, and your sister? What are you, Welsh?

No. She's actually just my wife. I only did it because I was afraid you would kill me and steal my wife if I told you we were married.

That makes no sense. What do you take me for, an animal? I've created the greatest empire the world has yet seen, built monuments and temples which will never be surpassed, I'm a man of distinction, I've showered you with goods and kindness... and all the while you lie to me? You disgust me, Abe.

What? said Abe, going on the offensive-defensive. So you want me to give you everything back now? Is that it? You were only my friend so you could sleep with my sister, eh?

Abe was terrified of losing everything, but luckily his offensive-defensive gamble paid off. Pharaoh was so disgusted by his friend's deceit, he just turned to him and said coldly: Go, keep it. Get out of my sight.

Can I get that in writing?

The look Pharaoh flashed Abe's way indicated he could not.

Like a speeding bullet, Honest Abe was off and running to his quarters.

Sarai, get the jewels and the fancy sandals – we're leaving.

What? But I love it here.

Look lady, when Honest Abe says it's time to haul ass, it's time to haul ass.

And like that, they were on their way, with all the wealth Abe had accumulated from Pharaoh.

As time went on, and they had made many other places their home, Sarai still had not conceived an heir.

How am I ever going to claim all that lucrative development land without an heir? Abe wondered.

This preyed on his mind so heavily, his penis refused to work and Abram became depressed, until one day, he felt joy in his heart, and other bits.

Hurrah for me and mankind, Abram said.

Abram was blessed with a son, and was overcome with relief and joy! *He* had been fine all along, it was

Sarai that had been the problem.

The only trouble was, he'd had to find this out through a control experiment – that is, honest Abe had knocked up the slavegirl, and she was the one with child, not Sarai.

It's a miracle, said Abram.

The hell it is, said Sara, dropping the 'i' in her name in a fit of rage. Steve Jobs entered stage left and picked it up, dusted it off then crept away across the sands to use it for his own nefarious purposes.

When God came upon the none-too-happy domestic scene, he perceived that Abram had created an heir.

The fecker, said God to Himself, I'd promised that land to someone else. Now I'll have to break My Word.

Though it was His own fault, God still felt enmity towards Abram for putting him in this position.

You know what, said God, appearing before Abram suddenly: I promised you all this land for your descendents, but in case you thought I wasn't going to give you any, I promise you now as many descendents as there are grains of sand on a beach, or stars in the sky. And they will undergo hard times and slavery for four hundred years before the first will see this promise fulfilled.

Abram considered that half a lifetime wasn't too bad, and said thanks once more. He could not know that God's promise would mean terrible overcrowding, not knowing what a beach was, and only being able to see a few thousand stars in the sky.

Ha, thought God: Let's see how 10^{24} people like living in this little shard of land.

However, God still felt dissatisfied, because Abram

didn't know he was getting shafted.

You know, said God: As a sign of my favour, you must cut off the foreskin.

The what now?

The skin on the end of your penis.

What about it? asked Abraham guardedly.

You must cut it off.

Why?

As a sign.

What?! said Abram. Wait, didn't you invent us?

I did, said God.

Then why not just leave off the foreskin in the first place?

No one likes too many questions, Abe, said God. Now, snip off the end of himself or you're getting nothing from me. Oh, and you've to do it for all your servants and sons, too. All the males.

Fuck's sake, muttered Abe, not too happy about the thought of interfering with everyone's man-bits.

I'm *sorry*?! said God.

Nothing, said Abe, I'll get sharpening the stone.

This deed done, Abram decided he would join his wife in a name change, and was thereafter known as Abraham, father of all the nations of the world.

SODOM & GOMORRAH

One day, as God was visiting Abraham, he chanced upon the nearby Sodom and Gomorrah, two towns full of debauchery and unspeakable things. Desperate things. If one can imagine Las Vegas during Spring Break, twinned with the seedier parts of Amsterdam, with a splash of 20's Paris, and twirl the *Class* dial waaay down, you're not even close: the things people got up to would make reality-tv stars look dignified.

After inspecting the two towns thoroughly, God was offended. To his core. He tsked and tut-tutted his way all across the desert floor until he came to Honest Abe's house.

He coughed to announce himself before entering the house.

Hail, God, said Abraham. Any chance of getting some of my descendents' land yet? I want to sow some runner beans and turnips.

Oh, leave it out, Abraham, God said, rubbing His eyes vigorously. I've just seen some terrible things.

Ah, been to Sodom, have you?

God shot him a keen look. How did you know?

Ah, said Abe lightly: A man hears things, is all. Sounds like harmless fun to me.

Well, I'm not you, Abraham. I'm Me, God. Almighty God Almighty, and I'm going to destroy them.

What? All of them? said Abraham.

Every last one of the deviants, said God.

Wait, what about the innocent ones, the good people.

There are none, replied the Creator, with a shudder of remembrance of things seen and indelibly burnt into a Memory that forgets nothing.

There must be.

There aren't, I tell you.

But if there were, would you let them live?

I never let innocent people die, said God. (The liar.)

If I can find fifty good men in the town, you won't destroy it, will you?

God said, Okay, for fifty good men, I might leave the town undestroyed.

Then Abe said, what about forty-five?

That's less than fifty, replied God. Bring on the drone strikes.

Wait Lord, said Abe. Please.

Fair enough, show me the forty-five.

Well, I don't have them yet, said Abe.

This negotiation went on for some time.

...If I can find ten, said Abraham. Ten good men. Ten, just ten. What about ten, Lord God?

For the love of Me, Abraham, will you ever give over; you're driving me crazy. Why didn't you say ten in the first place?

I like driving a bargain, said Abe: It's an important stereotype to pursue for my future descendents.

Whatever, said God. I'm sending in the Widowmakers.

Fine, said Abraham, but don't forget to warn the good guys.

Later that week, Abraham sent God his list of ten good men in the city of Sodom. Most of them were made up, but God still mostly trusted Man in those days, and sent two naked angels to forewarn the good guys and allow them time to evacuate the city before hellfire was rained upon the Godforsaken city.

The angels, masquerading as humans, went to the city of Sodom. Therein, they went to the home of Lot.

They knocked on the door, and the good man Lot opened it.

Yes? he said.

Hi Lot, wot? Got a lot, Lot? they asked.

It had been a long trip from Heaven and they had spent most of it making fun of Lot's name. (Angels are not very inventive, like all underlings. Archangels, on the other hand... that's another story, for another day.)

Come in come in, said Lot, looking furtively out the door as he shut it after them.

He covered them in spare cloaks. They were beautiful men, and naked as the day they were born, not that angels ever are, of course, but you get the idea. Lot feared for their safety, as he lived by the quays, a very up-and-coming neighbourhood but still dangerous, as the creative types had recently moved into the area in accordance with the scripture, but more aggressive seagoing types still populated the narrow brick-lined alleys, not to mention those more recently excused from prisons, neither of whom liked naked men wandering about the place.

Lot made some tea and cake for the angels.

So, what brings you to these parts, men? said Lot.

Lot–

You got–

To get–

Out.

So spake the angels, who then laughed at their rhyming brilliance.

What? said Lot, sending the angels into further peals of laughter.

A loud banging on the door put an end to their mirth.

Lot, who're those two buttercups I saw you bring in? said a voice outside the door.

Open this door, said another voice, or we're gonna bust it down and then bust you up.

High-fives were heard outside, and aggressive manly hollering, on account of this linguistic trickery.

Lot went to the door, and opened it a crack to peer outside.

Feck, said Lot, then turned back inside to address the two angels. They're after you two, he said to them.

What about my two virgin daughters? said Lot to the crowd outside.

Out of the way, Lot, we want those fairies, bayed the crowd.

Things were getting dangerous so the angels pulled Lot back inside and slammed the door, not before blinding the crowd outside with little laser lights on keyrings that God had entrusted them with.

After securing the door, the angels turned to see Lot's lusty daughters attempt to take advantage of him.

Away with ye, ye weird women, said Lot, pushing them off him: Now, gentlemen, what is going on?

Lot, we're here to destroy the city. It is full of sin. Get yourself and your family out. Take what you can but be gone by nightfall.

So saying, they focused their lasers on a small bed of straw in the corner and set flame to it. Lot fled to his other daughters, and respective sons-in-law, and tried to convince them to follow him, but to no avail.

He left, with his wife and the two weird daughters.

Now, none of you are to look back, said Lot, that's what the angels said.

Of course, his wife wouldn't listen to him, and was turned into a pillar of salt. Lot cried, then, being a practical man, gathered her into a canister and thought fondly of her every time he ate steak and chips. That was almost every day, as his daughters insisted he keep his energies up, before plying him with wine and having sex with him while he was in a drunken slumber.

Yes, truly, that was Lot's lot, as recorded in the good book. And *these* were the people worth saving from the city of Sodom?! Says it all, really.

In the meantime, Honest Abe got up the following day and looked out of his tent during his morning yoga, only to spy, with his little eye, something beginning with *A*.

Armageddon. End of days, for Sodom and Gomorrah, at any rate. And also for some investments that somebody had been conned into making in the up-and-coming quay neighbourhood in Sodom.

Feck, said Abe, then turned back to Sara, who still lay sleeping in their marital bed. He shook her awake.

Morning, Abe, she said sleepily.

Morning, he replied, as he began gathering things into a haversack. You know all that wealth Pharaoh gave me?

Gave *us*. What are you doing with our clothes?

Right. Well. He kinda gave the gold to me, but anyway… You know that development I told you about in Sodom?

That thing smelled fishier than month-old mackerel. I hope you didn't put any of our savings in it. What are you doing gathering up my jewellery?

My savings. Anyway, God went and smoked the entire town last night.

What?

I know. The bastard. Anyway, some people may be coming to me today for money I no longer have, so let's get on the move, shall we?

So saying, he threw a haversack to Sara and began filling another.

Within a half-hour, Abe and Sara were once again on the road, under assumed identities.

They came to Gerar, named for the roar of Lion.

The border official said, Welcome to Gerar.

Thank you, said Abe. This is my sister.

No one's asking, said the border official, looking at the centenarian beside the aged man.

Not this again, said Sara, throwing her eyes up to Heaven.

They were welcomed to Gerar by the king, who was also the border official. It was a small town. As a show of generosity, the king gave Sara the use of his own bedchamber. He also slept in the same room himself, there being nowhere else to sleep in the town except the front room where Abe was busily snoring.

Needless to say, the king of Gerar did not sleep with Sara. He was a virile twenty-seven year old male in the prime of his life and a king of his people. It stood to reason that he had his pick of the Gerarians, or Gerarish. Gerarites. The people of Gerar. They consisted of his wife and himself, who was currently visiting her cousin in nearby Herar.

Despite the absence of intercourse with Sara, God came to the king of Gerar in the morning and said: You're a dead man.

What? said the king, Who're you? Why?

You're a dead man. I'm God. For sleeping with Abe's wife, said God, answering all the questions put to Him.

That's not his wife, that's his sister, and I never touched her, clarified the border guard-king.

It's his wife, said God, and you were sleeping with her.

It's his sister, said the king, insistently, and unless you're getting very technical over the use of the word 'sleeping', I did not. Look, continued the king, to be quite clear, I did not have intercourse with that woman.

Monica Lewinsky? said God, with a puzzled look.

Who? said the king.

Nothing, said God, you were saying?

Look, said the king, I just want to do the right thing here. I did nothing to that old lady. Look at her, and at me.

So saying, the king flexed his muscles.

God, there's been a terrible mistake, he said.

God looked over and back between the healthy male and the old woman still sleeping in the corner of the room by the fire and realised his mistake, and silently blamed Abe, but to cover His error, said: Well, okay now, if you don't sleep with her–

I won't.

Yes, well if you don't, then you may live.

Fine.

Fine.

Fine, said the king.

Fine, said God and left in a huff, having had His Ass handed to him in a debating competition for the first time since... well, since nobody's business.

The next day, the king said to Abe: I had the weirdest dream last night, that someone came to me and said Sara is your wife.

She is my wife, said Abe, chewing his unleavened bread carefully, since he was almost a thousand and his teeth were not in good nick.

You said she was your sister, said the king.

That's also correct, said Abe, but only half-sister, so it's legal.

It's sick, said the king. What the hell is wrong with this part of the Bible?

What's the Bible? said Abe.

This is, said the king, punching him in the face. Now, any more questions?

No, but you remind me of Noah, said Abe, who then left with his wife-sister to go live in the kingdom of Gerar, while God was busy sending angels around to untie the womb of the king of Gerar's wife, which he had tied up in the first place to punish the king for a crime he did not commit.

Thereafter, thanks to some fertility treatment, Abe and Sara had a baby boy, whom they called Isaac. They were going to call him either Isaac or Pichsnot if it was a boy, and Drew or Barley if it was a girl.

Thanks be to God it was a boy, said Abe.

What was? asked Sara.

Isaac, he replied.

It came to pass that Sara died, not long after, in the overall scheme of things. Abraham missed her terribly and lavished lots of attention on their son, Isaac, now that the boy remained his last chance of inheriting all that development land.

One morning, God was bored, not having any four-dimensional chess to play, so he decided to have a bit of fun on Earth.

Now, then, he said, where is that Abraham fellow?

He found the multi-centenarian dozing beneath a

tree, and gave him a kick to wake him.

Abraham, you ould deaf codger, get up! said the Lord.

God Almighty, is it time?

Time for what?

Am I dead yet?

Don't be silly, I'm not done with you yet. Get your son Isaac–

My only true son and heir?

Yes, that one. Bring him to this mountain I want to show you, and burn him to death as an offering to me.

You're joking.

I am not.

Why in the name of You would I do that? Are You crazy?

Bored, really, but yes, in My Name shall you do it.

What if I don't?

I'll kill you.

Not if the bronchitis doesn't get me first. And God, the arthritis is something terrible, so it is. And my back; oh, the pain: I can tell if there's rain coming a week away, with the–

Listen, I am your Lord, I command you to do this.

Fine, You better not be kidding though.

What do you mean?

If I'm going to go through with this, You better not be messing around. I'll do this, but only because You asked.

I didn't ask; I commanded. I am your Lord–

Well, whatever You call yourself, I'm just saying You better not be kidding around.

God left in a huff. Those bloody ungrateful humans,

He said. Shut up you, Lion.

Lion, passing below, didn't even bother replying. There was a certain satisfaction to silent reproach.

So Abraham announced to Isaac that they were going on a picnic.

Gather up that timber, he said to his son, and carry it.

Abraham thought that there was a certain sadistic touch to this, like digging one's own grave, if that was even possible in this caked and meagre desert soil, which it wasn't.

Okay, said Isaac, and proceeded to heft his own murder weapon onto his back. Dad, aren't open fires forbidden in the park this time of year?

Bah, said Abraham, for want of a better response. Come on.

They made it into the mountains, Isaac helping his infirm old father up through the steep and rough terrain.

Here's a good place for it, said Abraham. Now, Isaac, put that timber down there and have a liedown on it, while your old dad makes us some lunch.

Isaac, weary from the climb, acquiesced.

Why do you sprinkle me with rosemary and petrol, father? Isaac asked.

Never you mind, said Abraham, raising a knife over his head to plunge it deep into his son's heart.

Whoa! said a voice.

It's an angel, said Abraham.

Dead Sea Park Ranger, actually, said Noah's successor. Now mind telling me what the hell is going on here?

Abraham dropped the knife and kicked it away beneath the timber.

The park ranger walked slowly towards them, sniffing the air. Is that… is that petrol I smell?

I told him, officer, said Isaac.

Whoa! What the shoot? said the ranger, spotting the boy atop the kindling for the first time. There's a kid up on this pyre… what is this, some kind of Satanic ritual? I'm gonna have to call this one in.

He reached for his weapon and trained it on Abraham while speaking to his shoulder walkie-talkie: Uh yeah, Sheila, we got a UFO here… No, U, U! No! U, as in… uh, uterus. Unsanctioned Fire Occurrence. Yes, UFO, Sheila, that's what I said. Look, send some backup, will you? The perp's an old man but he looks kind of crazy, and there may be a child to be taken into custody– I'll check, hold on. Sonny?

Yessir, replied Isaac.

Do you know this man, sonny?

I'm his only son and heir, sir.

Wait, that's not true, said Abe. Isaac, I have another boy. Well, man at this stage, he's probably a hundred years old already.

Wow, said Isaac. Oh, okay, I see what was going on here. Fine, burn me to death, Dad. See if I care.

Now, hold on, said the park ranger. No one's burning anything today. We've a 'no fire' restriction until the drought is over. Go home, both of you, he said, untying Isaac, and offering them a complimentary ham.

Isn't is supposed to be a ram? said Abe.

You want it or not? said the ranger.

Well, isn't pig flesh forbidden to us?

Not until later in the narrative, said the ranger. Enjoy, and remember, no fires until the drought's over.

So saying, he disappeared in a metaphorical and literal whirlwind.

That was weird, said Isaac.

You're telling me, said Abe, I could have sworn we had rain only yesterday. Now, gather up that firewood I was going to burn you on and bring it home. Don't you know how valuable that stuff is, or have I taught you nothing?

You have, said Isaac gratefully, now when do I get to meet my brother?

You can't, said Abe, I sent him and his mother into the desert to die for all I care.

You're not a nice guy, dad, are you?

My descendents inherit the Earth, said Abe. I am the chosen one.

Not long after, Abe took ill. Fearing the worst, he sent for his most faithful servant, Giles.

Sire? said Giles, entering the tent discreetly. He had been schooled in the butlery arts in a country estate in England, and knew how to do all sorts of things in the most correct manner.

Place your hand under my thigh and make a solemn vow to me.

With respect, sire, I'd rather place my hand upon my heart—

Get down on your knees and cup my thigh! blasted Abe, getting vicious.

Before you could say 'demeaning and degrading servitude' Giles was on his knees at his master's loins.

Now, said Abe to his most faithful servant, Isaac must have a wife.

What about one of these locals? said Giles.

I want to keep the bloodline pure, said Abe.

Toxic, more like, said Giles to himself, but simply observed: But sire, he has no sister, nor even a mother.

Ah, but he has cousins; they're almost like sisters in the eyes of the law.

True, said the servant.

Go now, said Abe, and fetch one of them for me.

For you? said Giles, looking at Abe's withered below-bits.

On my behalf, you clown, said Abe, for Isaac to marry.

Right, yes, of course, said Giles.

And lo, a dear, a female dear called Rebecca – Isaac's first cousin's daughter – was captured by Giles and brought back with tales of the extravagant wealth and development land that Isaac stood to accumulate.

Rebecca was a beauty, and a virgin, and no man had known her either, whatever that means. In any case, Rebecca was a catch from a looks point of view; Isaac from a financial point of view, so it was a match made in Heaven. Or at least, sanctioned by God in Heaven. And others in Heaven, such as Abe, who had by now made it up there, joining the illustrious company of Adam, Abel, Noah and the others in the VIP lounge in Heaven. Apart from Abel, who was busy whipping up flans and delicate pastries in God's kitchen.

JACOB

Years passed, and Isaac and Rebecca had still produced no offspring. Once more, there were… procreational difficulties with the line promised the Earth by God. He was crafty, the Lord God, one would have to say that about Him.

She's barren, said Isaac to his mates.

He's small and sterile, said Rebecca to her friends.

It was that kind of relationship. Poisonous from the off, and founded on mutual distrust.

Time had pushed on, and they found themselves both beyond the optimal age for making babies, and in bed trying to do exactly that.

No, Isaac, said Rebecca, repulsing his advances. Dr Reuben said we shouldn't do this at my age.

It's okay, baby, said Isaac. God told me we should.

Okay, then, she said. Well, if *He* said so…

And Isaac and Rebecca made love, and Isaac's seed was blessed, and Rebecca became with child.

Thirty-two weeks later, Rebecca was waddling about the house in great pain.

God, this hurts, she said aloud.

God, who was in the neighbourhood, overheard her and came in the door. Doors were left open in Biblical times – for one thing they weren't yet invented; for another, you could trust people more in those days.

Rebecca, said He.

God, how's it going? replied Rebecca.

You're pregnant, God observed.

You knew that already, said Rebecca.

What? How do you mean?

Isaac told me. This was Your idea.

The hell it was – you're nearly sixty years of age! Didn't you ask your doctor about this?

Well…

Well what?

I did, but Isaac said that You said that You thought it was a good idea.

And if Isaac told you that I told him that you should jump off a cliff, would you do it?

Wait, you told him to tell me to do what? replied Rebecca.

Oh, look, never mind, said God. Right well, let's have a look.

He used his laser Superman eyesight.

Hmmph, He said: Well, I can see why you're in discomfort.

What is it?

You've got twins. A big one and a little one, and they're fighting in the womb.

Stop that now, children, said Rebecca to her

stomach. We've company.

Nothing you can do about it, Rebecca, said God. They'll be at that til the end of their days, and what's more, the second fella will be a right bossyboots.

Ah no, really?

Well, said God, affronted, that's my verdict anyway, but what would I know, I'm not a doctor. I'm just God.

Point taken, said Rebecca meekly. Thanks God.

Once more, God left a conversation with a human, completely baffled by their casual attitude towards Him, their Creator. Rebecca sat back in discomfort and reflected on God's news as she chewed antacid tablets like candy.

Finally, the birth occurred of the twins. Out came number one, a hairy ginger.

God preserve us, said Rebecca, he has red hair. It must be a miracle.

My ass, muttered Isaac, knowing the reputation of local builder Paddy Flaherty. He stepped to the kitchen and took a knife from the drawer.

When he returned, their second son had appeared, this one having less hair and of a darker variety.

We're keeping the two of them, announced Rebecca sternly, looking at the knife her husband was wielding. Now, this first one is hairy, so we'll call him 'hairy', or Esau, in the local tongue.

Well that's lacks invention, said Isaac. And the other boy? said Isaac.

Jacob?

Fair enough, said Isaac. Now, I'm off to the pub to introduce Paddy Flaherty to my knife.

As they grew up, Esau turned into a hardy boy, off cavorting and cow-poking and hunting and fishing and killing. He spent all his days outdoors and naked. Jacob, by contrast, wore the finest of fabrics. He rarely left the comforts of the house behind and became skilled in backbiting and treachery.

Esau, as the eldest, was due to inherit everything from his father. As Isaac grew old and infirm, God took his sight, and a goodly portion of his hearing and mental faculties too, if what transpired is to be believed. What happened was this:

One day, while Esau was out in the desert stalking wild goats, Jacob and his mother tricked Isaac into blessing Jacob instead of Esau. Although Isaac was blind, he still had a wonderful nose and a delicate touch, so they faked Esau's hairiness and smell using goatskins and Old Spice.

When the deceit was complete, and the deeds were signed over to Jacob, Isaac realised he had been fooled. He was furious, but he was also very old, completely blind and utterly reliant on his wife for survival. Why Rebecca deceived her husband and her firstborn son remains a mystery, though the proliferation of ginger babies in the neighbourhood might have left her feeling sore. In any event, Esau returned that evening wearing a goatskin upon his shoulders, in great humour. His mood soured when he discovered the treachery, and not having access to a good lawyer to protect his rights, swore instead to kill Jacob.

Rebecca overheard Esau plotting in his room. She scuttled next door to Jacob, who was busy posing in front of a mirror and trying on his new clothes.

Jacob, said Rebecca, you're going to your cousins in Haran.

I don't want to. Those guys are so uncivilised, said Jacob.

Do as you're told, you little brat, said his mother, swatting him about the ears. I'm doing this for your own good.

With that, she set him off down the street for the Haran Express with a note in his hand for the cousins in Haran, and a stinging arse from the wooden spoon for daring to question her authority.

En route, Jacob fell asleep and had a dream about a ladder, with angels going up and down to Heaven on it. He interpreted the ladder as his penis and the angels as little spermatozoa, and further postulated that this meant he should marry two of his first cousins when he got to Haran, and their two slave girls, and have sex and babies with the lot of them.

(Millennia later, the likes of Sigmund Freud would have a field day with this, but nonetheless Jacob was a firm believer in following your dreams, even the weirdly incestuous ones. In his defence, he was only following family protocol since at least Honest Abe's time.)

Before long, Jacob had indeed succeeded in marrying two of his first cousins and their slave girls in Haran, then snuck away from his uncle's farm in the dead of night with a flock of his uncle's goats and Jacob's own various children and wives-slash-lovers.

Rachel, one of his official wives-slash-cousins, stole valuables from her father's house, for kicks. When Rachel's father finally caught up with the ne'er-do-wells, God materialised and warned him not to be annoying poor little Jacob and his family.

But God, protested Jacob's uncle and father-in-law, this little bastard here – who I took into my own house, gave the very best of food and drink to, and clothed – he stole from me, snuck off, had sex with multiple women, married multiple times... I mean, there's felonies here, probably half of the ten commandments broken–

Who told you about the Ten Commandments? thundered God.

No one. I hear some things.

Begone! shouted God, and leave poor Jacob alone.

Jacob, standing behind God, stuck his tongue out at his uncle and ran chuckling back to his harem.

Come on, bitches, said Jacob, we're off to claim my inheritance.

(Yes, Jacob was a real piece of work.)

Jacob and his family then returned to his motherland. Esau, Jacob's hirsute brother, had lived there all his life and had married a local girl completely unrelated to him, which made him somewhat of a pariah amongst his family. He worked an honest living and had a reputation as an upstanding member of the community, though he was a little too fond of the drink, which some blamed on his 'heritage, if you know what I mean'. This phrase was usually accompanied by some prodding of the elbow towards the conversant's ribs.

Esau was none too charmed by the thought of the return of his incestuous pimp-brother.

He's going to bring prostitution and drugs into our community, said Esau in the pub.

Let's stone him, said his fellows in the bar.

There and then, it was determined that they would kill Jacob. However, Jacob arrived just at that moment. With an inbuilt hide-saving instinct, he bought numerous rounds of drink for everybody, until all plans to kill him had been drowned in brandy. Esau decided to let bygones be bygones, and announced that he and Jacob would drink to forgiveness. Jacob was not much of a drinker, but he saw the sense in making peace with his strong and influential brother. To be polite, he suggested a further toast, to celebrate being brothers. Then another followed, and another, to celebrate being brothers who were at peace, and world peace, and living forever, and being great specimens of manhood.

That night, Jacob had no idea how he managed to get home, but he told Rachel that he had dreamt a dream that he fought an angel. Or God. He was unclear on the details afterwards, only that he had somehow damaged his hip.

The angel did it, he claimed.

My foot, Jacob. I saw you falling, said Rachel. You were drunk as a skunk.

The angel–

My foot! said Rachel. You're not going to end up like Esau. I'm checking you into rehab and that's that.

That very day, Rachel booked Jacob into the local Cleanout Clinic.

Six months passed, and Rachel paid the monthly bill from the Clinic on time every time. At length, she decided to visit her husband to see if he had any intention of ever leaving.

Hello, she said at the door, I've come to see how my husband is doing.

You tell me, said the proprietor, he left four months ago.

What? What the hell am I paying you for?

Well, he still sleeps here on occasion, but he has a tab set up in half the pubs in town and they're billing us directly, so we're billing you.

Bulling me, more like, muttered Rachel, determined that this would be the end of that sort of carry-on.

The next morning, his head still pounding from his hangover, Jacob was checked in to the exclusive remote mountain resort Mekubedder Clinic, run by pre-Christian monks.

One month later, after fighting his inner demons and battling the drink, Jacob arrived home and announced he had changed his name to Israel.

I hope you're joking, said Rachel.

I am not, what's wrong with Israel?

What's wrong with Jacob?

Nothing, just–

A slap across his face stopped him talking.

You'd want to cop on to yourself, Jacob or Israel or whatever you call yourself, said his wife-slash-cousin Rachel. You have at least twelve children from four different women, and you're still wandering around the desert like some itinerant beggar, never having done a stroke of work all your life.

They didn't speak for a week afterwards, as Israel mulled over these hard-hitting home-truths. Not long after, they had make-up sex. Not long after that, Rachel became pregnant once more, and Jacob decided the family were going to move, this time to the up-and-coming suburbs on the outskirts of Bethlehem.

Rachel grumbled about the move as she waddled about the house neatly labelling all their removal boxes: …I mean, the timing, Jacob. Look at me, I'm pregnant, didn't you consider me?

Honestly, Rachel, said Israel, this will be the last time you have to move, I promise.

He wasn't kidding. Shortly after moving to Bethlehem, Rachel gave birth to another boy, Benjamin, then died. Israel was distraught, but had learnt a lot about philosophy and the circle of life while in rehab, so he coped. He had to, having twelve hungry boys to feed, including the newest – Benjamin – as well as Rachel's eldest and his personal favourite, Joseph.

JOSEPH

Now, Joseph, as Israel-nee-Jacob's favourite, was given a fancy jacket by his father Israel-nee-Jacob (hereinafter called only Israel for the avoidance of confusion, although some of his personal correspondence was still addressed to *Jacob*, which caused no end of heartache for the local postmistress). The other brothers were jealous of Joseph and his coat, fearing that if ever their useless father was to make something of himself like their wealthy uncle Esau, then most-popular-son Joseph would get left everything in the will.

So one day, after Joseph was telling his brothers about a dream he had had, they threw him down a well, then drew him back up and sold him into slavery to a passing caravan, for thirty-five currency units, a goodly number. Thirty-five was seven times five, both auspicious numbers in their burgeoning religious tradition, seven and five adding to twelve, the number of brothers; seven minus five equalling two, the number of brothers in their father's family; and twelve divided by two being six, a combination of three times two, two being the number of threes required to make six, a holy number. It all made sense if you thought about it for too long.

Joseph's brothers returned to Israel with Joseph's coat, covered in blood from a lamb, and said: Look, father, your son is dead.

And he got lambsblood on that expensive coat I got him, too, the little bastard, said Israel, in a fit of temper: Oh God, why have you allowed this to happen?

Israel got over his sadness, though, as more important things had happened elsewhere. His own father Isaac had died, aged one hundred and eighty, a sacred number in the cult of darts.

Some locals queried whether Isaac had falsified his birth cert, arguing that physiologically it was impossible to live beyond about one hundred years even with the best medical care, but Esau and Israel said it was all in the genes, and that their ancestor Noah had lived to over eight hundred.

Now, Israel came to claim dominion over his brother Esau once the will was announced. Not the will of God the Father, but the will of their lowercase father, Isaac.

However, it transpired that Isaac had given everything he owned to the Brothers of Charity and their orphanage, so he had the last laugh on both of his sons, the crafty old codger. This led to the saying 'never trust a blind man of one hundred and eighty'. This saying was later interpreted by scholars as having something to do with Masonic lore, and was not to be read literally.

After mourning the death of his father Isaac and the trickery of the will, Israel returned to his grief over his son Joseph, and was miserable.

In the meantime, Joseph (sans multi-coloured frockery) had made his way on the caravan towards Egypt. Playing at dice and gambling, he earned enough to buy his way out of slavery and furthermore to pay for a decent education, whereupon he entered the service of Pharaoh's captain of the guard, Pat O'Fur.

Pat O'Fur was only ever concerned with getting a feed of cabbage and chips at the end of his working day, so he left the administration of his considerable property empire to Joseph.

As happens all men, Joseph began to consider that everything he administered actually was his own, including Pat O'Fur's wife.

One day, having attempted to have his way with Mrs O'Fur, Joseph found himself thrown into prison, accused of having attempted to have his way with Mrs O'Fur.

While sitting in the cell, the door opened.

Joseph looked up. Pharaoh's baker and Pharaoh's butler walked in.

Is this some sort of joke? asked Joseph.

If it is, I'm not laughing, said the baker miserably.

I wouldn't blame you, said Joseph, you're going to be hanged.

What?! said the baker. Why?

No wait, said Joseph hurriedly, that bit comes after the dream.

What dream? said the baker.

Nothing, said Joseph, and turned away from him and huddled on his prison bed shivering, with a meagre sheet pulled over him. Not that it was cold – Egypt in the summer doesn't exactly require thick duvets and bedspreads – but Joseph had a point to make.

Let me out of here, Joseph said to the jailer.

Give me one good reason why I should.

I'm innocent.

That's a good reason, said the jailer approvingly, nodding his head.

So, can I get out?

No, but it's still a good reason.

With that, the jailer threw gruel against the wall and let the three prisoners lick their food off it.

The butler cried, then sighed, then tried to cry and sigh at the same time, then choked, then recovered, then licked gruel off the wall. All of this took about fourteen seconds.

Why did you do that? asked Joseph suspiciously, then innocently, to see the difference. There was none.

The butler cleared his throat, and said: I have a dream–

Not yet, hissed the off-stage prompter, you have to go to sleep first.

Right, yes, of course, hissed the butler in reply.

Hiss, hissed a snake intended as a prop to add danger to the scene.

Right, said the butler, I'm about to turn in for the night.

Me too, said the baker.

Oh alright, then, me too, said Joseph, after strangling the snake with his bare feet.

The next morning, the baker and the butler both looked sad.

Why the long faces? asked a pantomime horse, to

general ignorance.

Joseph woke some time later, to find the baker and the butler looking glum.

Why the long faces? he asked.

I already asked that, said the horse, to specific ignorance.

Well, began the butler, I had a dream, and in that dream there were three grapes that I squeezed into the cup of Pharaoh.

And you, baker? said Joseph.

Well, said the baker, I too had a dream, and in that dream there were three wheat stalks and they all died.

It's your lucky day, said Joseph to them, for I am a champion dream interpreter. Butler, your dream means that within three working days, excluding the Sabbath and the day following, you shall be back working for Pharaoh.

Hurrah, said the butler.

Hurrah, said the baker.

Not so fast, you! said Joseph to the baker. Your dream means that you're going to be hung within three days because the bread you made caused Pharaoh to fall ill.

It was the yeast, protested the baker.

It was Colonel Mustard with the candlestick, retorted Joseph. No one gives a damn, so say your prayers and prepare to meet your maker, baker.

Joseph's interpretations cast a gloom over the cell, what with the baker being warned of his impending death and all that.

Nonetheless, all that he said came to pass: the baker was put to death, and the butler was set free and proceeded to set up a very successful vineyard with a Michelin-starred restaurant by the banks of the Nile. However, the butler forgot all about poor Joseph, who languished in prison for many more years.

Joseph managed to fashion a tincup from loose bars in his window and used this to rattle across the bars into the main section of the prison, annoying the pantomime horse and other prisoners, and inventing spirituals to verbalise his inner angst, like the following:

> Down in old Pharaoh's land, (he sang)
> far from the land where I was born,
> they did throw me down, Lord,
> they did throw me down.
>
> Oh, down by that old Nile river, Lord,
> far from the land where I was born.
> They tore my clothes and cast me
> down, Lord,
> They tore my clothes and cast me
> down.

That's enough, cried the butler, entering the prison with a big key.

Oh hello, said Joseph, I'm preparing for my lead role in the prison play tonight.

Not any more, you're not, said the butler. I have caused you to be released.

I don't want to be released anymore, said Joseph. I like it here.

Tough, said the butler.

Hurrah, said the pantomime horse, who was Joseph's

understudy.

Oh mischievous Fate, cruel mistress! said Joseph, throwing himself against the gruel wall, hamming it up so that the other prisoners would get one last glimpse of what they would be missing in tonight's performance.

Now, stop that, said the butler. Come along with me, Pharaoh had a frightening dream and no one can interpret it.

Really? said Joseph, you just make stuff up. People will believe anything you tell them.

But… but you correctly predicted my dream, said the butler.

To a point, said Joseph. I just did that to impress you. All I really did was tell the jailer that the baker had confessed to spoiling your wine deliberately, so he took the rap for your crime and you got off scot-free.

You bastard! The baker was my brother, said the butler.

No need to sound so ungrateful, said Joseph in a hurt tone. Now, take me to this Pharaoh and I'll work my old black magic on him.

Not yet, said the guard, grabbing Joseph's arm. Have you forgotten that Pharaoh has an obsessive fear of bodily hair? Shaven or singed?

I'll have a singe, if it's all the same.

Be my guest, said the guard, escorting him to the fire-room. Don't stay in there too long if you don't want to look like a flaming tangerine.

I wasn't born yesterday, said Joseph laughing.

Nor was I, replied the guard. What's your point?

I don't have one, said Joseph, then went to sit by the fire until his hair had all burnt away.

He emerged from the fire-room one hour later, toasty and hair-free.

There we are, he said. Now, let me go meet Pharaoh.

Pharaoh sat restlessly on his throne, troubled by his dream and a bad case of piles.

Joseph came before him: Greetings Pharaoh, I have come to interpret your royal dream.

Good, said Pharaoh, what took you so long? My dream is as follows: Seven animals came from the river, healthy. Then seven more, weak and malnourished, and these devoured the healthy ones whole.

Alright– began Joseph.

Wait, said Pharaoh, I'm not done yet. I had a second dream, in which there were seven ears of corn upon a stalk, healthy, and then seven withered upon another stalk, and the seven withered ate the seven healthy ones.

Joseph said nothing.

Well? said Pharaoh.

Oh, said Joseph, I didn't know if you had more dreams.

No, that was it, just the two.

Okay, said Joseph, I'll tell you what; I'll charge you a group rate for the two dreams, seeing as how they're essentially the same dream.

Seems fair, said Pharaoh.

At this stage, a small fat man burst into the throne room. It's about your mother, he cried, you have unresolved sexual longing for her–

Guards! Throw that clown Freud out of here, commanded the captain of the guard, and two guards dragged Freud away, as the psychoanalyst frothed at the mouth.

So, said Joseph, it's like this: The dream means that there are seven animals in all the land that bear the mark of the golden ruler. Only one man in all the kingdom can distinguish that mark, and that man is me. Behold! I am in the service of God, and I alone can be called upon to know these beasts. If these seven bullocks be not brought forth by me, they shall surely trample down the land, and bring famine and disgrace to your nation, along with strife and bloodshed–

And what of the other beasts? asked Pharaoh.

I was getting to that, said Joseph. Seven virgin maidens are there, in all the land, that bear the mark of the golden ruler. Only one man etc etc famine and disgrace to your nation etc etc–

And the wheat?

The what?!

The wheat.

Oh yes, the wheat, thought Joseph to himself. Give me a minute, I'll think of something.

Ahahahaaaa! he cried aloud, and Pharaoh and the court fell back at this dreadful utterance.

The wheat, continued Joseph, clearly represents the thirteen–

There were only seven–

–the *thirteen*, I said, holy incantations known only to me–

This is nonsense, interrupted Pharaoh. This man is a charlatan, throw him back in prison.

Wait, cried Joseph in desperation, as two guards grabbed him. I have an MBA from Harvard–

What's Harvard? said one of the guards.

Not now, said Joseph, then turned back to the Egyptian ruler. Pharaoh, I know how to manage large institutions, such as your country, returning them to profitability – often at the expense of the common people, but to the benefit of those at the top. Pharaoh, let me be acting CFO of your company... I mean, country.

What's a CFO? asked a guard.

Oh you asked for it this time, said Joseph, laying him to the floor with an uppercut. That is, he said. Any more questions?

Pharaoh beamed down at Joseph: Harvard?! Why didn't you say so, my dear boy. Why, you're the perfect man to bring this country to the brink of financial ruin.

With that, Pharaoh anointed Joseph with oil, dressed him in vestures of fine linen and tweed, and gold jewellery about his neck.

There, said Pharaoh.

You don't think the gold is a bit blingy? asked Joseph.

Nonsense, said Pharaoh. It's a classy touch.

And just like that, Joseph was defacto ruler of Egypt, and he was but thirty years of age.

Ha, said Joseph to himself. A short time hence, I was in prison, in stifling heat, shivering in a meagre blanket for added pathos, and now look at me: controller of Egypt and looking forward to the ten-year class reunion like nobody else. Take that, Patterson and Lubowitz!

Joseph entered into his role with gusto, and aplomb, and a diamante-fringed necktie. He expropriated one-fifth of all property in the state, including the best fields.

What are you doing to my people? said Pharaoh. I hear about these things in the media.

It's okay, Pharaoh, said Joseph. Trust me, you'll be richer than ever.

And though Pat O'Fur, the chief of police, grumbled and watched Joseph like a hawk, he couldn't penetrate Joseph's obscure accounting practices enough to make a charge of misappropriation of public funds stick.

The next seven years were amongst the most profitable of all of Egypt's long and storied history. During this time, Joseph stockpiled and stockpiled, buying up all the grain that came on the market. Pharaoh demanded a greater payout of dividend, but Joseph stood firm.

Finally, a famine came, and Joseph was vindicated in his decision. People were forced to buy up his grain at multiples of what he had paid for it.

Told you so, said Joseph to Pharaoh. I'll make you wealthier than in your wildest dreams.

I don't know, said Pharaoh. I have some pretty wild dreams.

INTERLUDE, BEING THE MOST CURIOUS TALE OF JUDAH

One of Israel's sons, Judah, got himself a wife, Hirah, and then another, Shuah. These wives gave him three sons: Er (who was probably an accidental baby), and Onan, and Shelah (who was a boy despite his name).

Then Er married a woman called Tamar, but the

Lord God didn't like the cut of his jib, and killed him.

Judah said to his other son Onan: Boy, go in there and sleep with your brother's wife.

And Onan said: Who do you think I am, Ryan Giggs?

Just do what you're told, you disrespectful boy.

But Onan did not. He went into the tent with his sister-in-law.

Wow, said Onan to Tamar, you still have Er's body in the tent.

Yes, said Tamar, I find it comforting.

I find it disturbing, said Onan, then masturbated in a corner of the tent rather than sleeping with his recently-bereaved sister-in-law.

A twisted but noble act, one might consider.

The Lord God did not, however, and once again He killed in the night.

When Judah found Onan dead in the morning, he was distraught. He said to Tamar: Lady, you are cursed in some fashion. Best if you weren't around any more, what with my third-born Shelah–

The girl? said Tamar.

Shelah's not a girl, insisted Judah. My wife liked the sound of the name, is all. Anyway, with my last son still alive, it would be best if you weren't around. Go back to your father's house as a widow.

Tamar did not. She felt aggrieved by the way in which the whole matter was handled. She decided she wasn't done yet with Judah and his family. Finding out that they had moved to another neighbourhood, she followed them, dressed as a hooker and stood by the road crossing where she knew Judah would pass to tend to his sheep in the mountains.

Judah passed her by and thought: Ooh, it's a lonely life, it is, being a shepherd. I've a good mind to have a bit of flesh or one of the sheeps will get it.

How much? he said to his disguised daughter-in-law.

For what? she asked.

Sex.

What'll you give me?

A kid.

I don't want one; you'll be wearing a leather prophylactic.

No, a baby goat.

The hell with that, she replied. Give me all your jewellery.

Sounds reasonable, he said. Judah mostly wore costume jewellery and knock-offs, the trickster.

An accord reached, Judah and his disguised widowed daughter-in-law were in over an adjacent wall, trousers down, skirts up, and prophylactic in place.

Although Tamar had a revenge masterplan, she forgot what it was after her encounter with Judah and fled the neighbourhood. The following day, Judah observed that the hooker he had encountered yesterday had moved on. He asked around everywhere furtively, but could find no trace of her. Over time, he became obsessed, nailing up pictures of her to every low stone wall he could find, randomly sobbing in the day, but all in vain. Months passed, until one day Judah was informed that his daughter-in-law was prostituting herself.

Disgraceful, he said, spitting out the word. Pah, what a low and vile woman, that Tamar. You know what? She should be burnt to death. Wouldn't be half good enough for her. Prostitution, God Almighty. What is the world coming to?

Unfortunately for the misogynist hypocrite, it was a rare moment of tolerance and liberalism in history. Tamar demanded an open trial, and the key piece of evidence was her womb, which contained twins that she swore were her father-in-law's children. Judah, sensing which way the wind was blowing on this, quietly dropped charges and paid off the newspapyruses to hush up the scandal. He formally but secretly acknowledged paternity and provided for Tamar and his offspring. He also launched an unsuccessful lawsuit against the manufacturers of the prophylactic device that had failed him.

Tamar then had twins, one of whom stuck his hand out at the birth. The midwife, rather than attempting to birth the child, tied a scarlet ribbon to his wrist, then the child went back into the womb, only to be born second. She was a poor midwife, not in financial terms, but in midwifery, having come bottom of her class, and only being awarded a certificate in the end when she threatened to expose the entire college as a sham. It was indeed a confusing time in the Biblical tale, so it's probably best to return to Israel and his happy home.

CONCLUSION OF INTERLUDE

Except it wasn't a happy home.

Back at Israel's ranch, the famine hit hard. Neighbours mentioned that a family as large as Israel's *might* get

THE HOLIEST BIBLE EVER: BEING GOD

sustenance in Egypt (not that they were commenting on the size of his family, but if he *could* keep his third leg strapped to his thigh instead of dipping it into every pot of honey it encountered, he might be better able to provide for his family).

The truth was, Israel's farm, where all his sons were working, was destined to fail. They were lazy boys, it was south-facing and wouldn't have caught a drop of rain back in Noah's day, as the joke went.

Israel decided in a moment of bravado that he would blow the last of the family's money on a sun holiday to Egypt.

It'll be nice, he said to them, to get away from all this doom and gloom surrounding the farm and this famine.

Everyone packed their children and sandbuckets and prepared to set off across the desert, apart from Israel himself, who stayed behind to try to sell his property, and Benjy, the youngest boy.

Now, here's some money, said Israel to his sons: Bring me and Benjy back some corn so we don't starve to death.

And a swizzle stick and a stick of rock, added Benjy.

Quiet you, said Israel.

Daddy, why can't I go? asked Benjy.

In case something happens to you, his father replied.

Why would something happen him and not us? asked one of the other boys.

It wouldn't, but Benjy here happens to be my favourite since Joseph died.

Unbelievable, another son muttered, but being hungry, he didn't stick around complaining for long.

Arriving in Egypt, they booked into a nice motel on the edge of town: The Cleopatra, it was called, though no one knew why.

They visited the local vineyards, including one with a Michelin-starred restaurant, where the owner-slash-butler engaged them in conversation.

You guys from out of town, hey? Yes yes, the famine, we heard. Dreadful, simply dreadful, he said to them. Now, foie gras for starters, or we have some lovely grain-fed chicken cooked in rich butter?

In discourse, Israel's sons learnt that they would have to go to Pharaoh's CFO to get permission to ship grain abroad.

The next day, they arrived at the CFO's premises. Entering his luxuriously-appointed private sauna, the brothers bowed before Joseph. They did not recognise him, as he had had a foreskin grafted onto his member to blend in amongst the locals. Oh, and he was wearing a disguise, spoke Coptic, and hadn't seen his brothers for over a decade, all of whom had every reason to presume he was dead. Joseph certainly recognised them, though, and wasn't above having a little fun with them to compensate for his years of hardship after they had sold him into slavery.

Greetings, plebs, said Joseph. From whence came ye?

From Canaan, they replied.

Ha, you shit-eating bum-dirt monkey-face-kissers! Joseph said. Am I not correct?

Yes, your Grace, they replied, not enjoying the humiliation, but needing that grain.

You stinky-bottom stupids.

Yes, your Grace.

You knickers-wearing nose-pickers.

Yes, your Grace.

This went on a while. Revenge a la tartare, it was called.

At length, Joseph ran out of names to throw at them.

Very well, dirty-sock eaters, what do you want?

Grain, and a glass of water.

Let it be done, said Joseph. The going rate is all the money you have plus the brother that is not with you.

How did you know about him? asked Reuben, the eldest.

Silence! thundered Joseph. You are spies.

This guy's schizo, muttered another. Let's get out of here and just steal the grain we need.

Guards, lock these men up.

And like that, they were thrown into prison and the key thrown away.

In those days, lockmaking was in its infancy as a craft, and any lock could be picked in the time it took to turn a handle, being mostly decorative, but it was the principle of the matter. One had to stay inside the prison.

After a few days in the clanger, Joseph relented, and brought them before him.

Now, he said, all of you may return to your stinky-poo land but one, whom I shall keep as a surety of your return. Bring back the little kid, or the hostaged fellow shall die.

This they did, and Joseph was delighted to see his younger brother Benjy.

Having made up their differences, the boys returned home to fetch Israel and relocate the entire family in the manner of upwardly mobile immigrants for millennia.

Just as Israel and the boys were preparing to depart the desert forever, God arrived in a cloud.

Jacob, said God.

It's Israel nowadays, said Israel.

Say what now?

I changed my name to Israel.

You did what?

I prefer to be called Israel now.

God ignored this for the time-being and focused on the immigration underway: Where do you think you are going?

We're moving to Egypt: the climate's better, they have decent food, culture, and a great medical system. I'm getting old, God, and I no longer want the simple things in life. I want the best that money can buy. Joseph's money, in fact.

Hmm, said God, can't argue with that. Tell you what, I'll come with you.

Oh, you don't have to, said Israel.

What do you mean?

They have their own god. His name's Pharaoh, and my boy Joey is friends with him, actually. You don't need to come. You're a god of the desert; the city would just cramp Your style.

How dare you! said the Deity of the Desert. I'm God, the Almighty, the All-Powerful, the Al–

Alrighty then, said Israel. Breaking up is so very hard to do, God, but I'm off to the Egyptians – where they pay cash, not promises – and you're not coming. Don't wait up.

You bastards will be back, you'll see... muttered the Lord God bitterly, as he watched the caravan of people and trinkets snake out across the desert and hightail it for the pre-Cairo city of the Egyptians. ...And when you do, you'll suffer in the miserable Arabian Desert for generations as compensation for this betrayal.

Leaving their old ways and their old God behind, the Hebrews arrived to a tremendous welcome from Joseph, who put them up (at the country's expense) just a little outside Cairo, near the Cleopatra Motel complex, by now expanded to include a luxury hotel, conference centre, financial district, all-night shopping bazaar, and a garment factory where slaves worked morning noon and night on multicoloured garments known as josephs.

EXODUS, OR MOSES

It was many years after the time of Joseph ben-Jacob-slash-Israel, and the Israelites had been busy multiplying at a ferocious rate.

If we continue like this, it won't be long before we have our own representative in Parliament, said one Hebrew.

Of course, Parliament did not exist as yet. The current system of governance was Pharaonic rule, which meant that whatever Pharaoh said was law. Even if he'd been munching on strange berries, or wines of the Nile.

Indeed, right at this moment, Pharaoh was suffering from wines of the Nile. He had a tremendous hangover, and was taking the air along the Nile on a giant dhow to aid recovery.

Aaargh, he cried. Turn down the sun, my eyes burn.

His advisors looked at one another, unsure what to do.

Are you idiots deaf? he screamed. I said *turn down the*

sun. Immediately!

Ill-advisedly, one advisor stepped forward and whispered: Master, the Sun God Ra cannot be turned up or down.

Silence, cried Pharaoh in anguish, why are you shouting at me? Guards, take this man, kill him, then throw him to be drowned.

His order, in reverse order, was done. No other advisor spoke, and Pharaoh slumped back in his chair. A loud hubbub affected him from the riverside.

What the heck is that noise? he said.

Pharaoh, that is the Israelite quarter, answered an advisor.

Hmmm, the Israelites, mused the Egyptian ruler. Look at the size of those palaces they have built, and see how their population grows large.

He thought to himself for a while, then commanded: Make them slaves, and have them build palaces like that for me.

His word was made law, yet the Israelites continued to multiply under the burden of slavery, having little-or-zero spending money for prophylactics, or even for other forms of entertainment.

By now, Pharaoh was both more consistently sober and fully intent on curbing the influx of beggars, immigrants and do-gooder reformers seeking a change in how the land was governed. This very moment, he was disturbed by what he was hearing from an overseas emissary.

…so the Athenians all have the right to speak– said the visitor.

And what does their king say to this rabble? asked Pharaoh, understandably confused.

They have no king, Pharaoh. They are a democracy.

Come come, said Pharaoh. There must be someone in charge.

Bunch of bloody Communists, muttered Akhtopeth, his favoured advisor, at which the court burst into laughter.

If there's no one in charge, why don't I take charge? asked Pharaoh.

His military advisor stepped forward.

Pharaoh, their land is marginal at best, and doesn't benefit from the rich abundance of the silt of the Nile.

Coward, muttered Akhtopeth, and once more laughter rang around the court.

Later that same evening, Akhtopeth was assassinated by the court jesters, assisted by the military advisor, for threatening their livelihoods, which is a warning to all not to overstep the bounds of their employment, for toes might be trod upon in the darkness outside one's own lighted path.

Pharaoh had his own troubles that evening: his mind was filled with portentous dreams of the masses rising up, fuelled by the earnest speech of the man he had conversed with earlier that day. Through sheer force of numbers, they might overthrow his rule.

He decided upon two-pronged action: firstly, to pursue R&D in a covert project codenamed Ra's Wrath, which was the development of a ray-gun, focussing the sun's ray through a lens atop a pyramid onto a crowd of people, spontaneously turning them to ashes; secondly, to insist that all the male-born immigrant kids be killed.

A harsh measure, but as his father had warned him, the danger comes from the masses.

—and the assassins, Pharaoh Sr had said: Or small groups of people. Or those you love. In short, trust no one, my only son... he had uttered, as he lay dying from a knife wound to the abdomen, administered by his only son, who had grown tired of awaiting his turn to rule.

The ray-gun was surely Pharaoh's best means of controlling the population; however, until development of that was complete, he would have to continue with cackhanded interim measures, like insisting upon male infanticide amongst the immigrants.

The immigrant midwives were tasked with this, but they were bad citizens of the country into which they had been made welcome, and disobeyed Pharaoh's command.

Pharaoh, said Nehumtup, that didn't work; there's more immigrants than ever before.

Ah heck! said Pharaoh, looking at his signed copy of *Manual for Autocracy* by the Sphinx. He scrolled down to *Chapter 7: Dealing with Immigrants*.

Pharaoh was silent a moment, his lips moving as he traced the hieroglyphs with his fingers on the papyrus.

He had the midwives brought before him for this act of civil disobedience, but when questioned, they claimed the babies were delivered before they could get there.

Ah for Seth's sake, said Pharaoh to them. What is your purpose in that case?

This was a valid question, but one with no real answer, so Pharaoh received only sullen silence.

Pah, get out of here, you two, said Pharaoh.

The two midwives left, thanking their lucky stars (Kim Kardashian and the North Star, respectively).

After his meeting with the uncooperative midwives, Pharaoh commanded Nehumtup that, henceforth, all Hebrew male babies were to be thrown into the river.

A Hebrew man called Amram had a wife, Jochebed. As was traditional, Jochebed was also a blood relation of Amram, an aunt in this case. After they had made love, Amram's auntie-slash-wife gave birth to a baby boy, but when she threw him into the river, the infant swam away downstream and climbed onto some detritus at a bend in the river.

Sweet Jesus, said Jochebed. Did you see that?

I'm not Jesus, I'm Moses, replied the baby Moses, as he fashioned some reeds into an oar and steered his way down the Nile.

Further downstream, Pharaoh's daughter was by the river, watching as her pet crocodile Charlie gorged on a rich diet of babies.

When Pharaoh's daughter spotted Moses, she first feared the child might blind Charlie with the reeds he held in his fist. Then she took pity on the infant and took him into her care, lavishing every kindness upon him.

Many years later, proving that there is nothing so ungrateful as a spoilt child, and that you really can do nothing for some people, Moses was out and about one day when he came across an Egyptian whipping an

Israelite. Having checked to see that no one was watching, Moses killed the Egyptian.

Perfidious bastard, cry the Egyptians.

Huzzah, shout the Israelites.

Uh-oh, said Moses, I think I just made a big boo-boo.

Moses decided he had better flee Egypt for the present, what with a major manhunt across the nation for the Egyptian Egyptian-killer. That very night, he packed a sandwich, a banana and a flask of tea (with a jar of asses' milk to add in later, because it doesn't taste right if you add it too soon). Then, taking leave of his homeland, Moses fled into the night.

A week later, Moses was hanging out by a well in the desert, wondering what to do with his life, when seven sisters arrived. They got chatting, and Moses helped them to draw water from the well using his muscles. This kind deed was rewarded with another, when the father of the seven girls, Reuel, sent for this strong man and gave him one of the daughters to marry.

Which one? asked Moses.

Like I give a damn, said Reuel. I can't afford the dowry for any of them, being but a poor farmer, so take your pick, help out with the livestock and we'll get along fine, you and I.

In line with fine Biblical tradition, Reuel felt his name didn't really define who he was as a person, so he changed it to Jethro and became a priest.

Moses, meanwhile, had his own problems to contend with. Each of the seven sisters was throwing themselves at him, and Reuel-Jethro was doing nothing to prevent them, so Moses resorted to taking off for months at a time into the desolation of the desert with the sheep.

Amidst this wilderness, having been without water for days, God appeared to him, in a burning bush. No LSD was consumed, although in his search for moisture, Moses may have eaten some strange brightly-coloured roots.

God! said Moses. Dude!

Moses, are you drunk? said God.

Duu-uuude, replied Moses.

That's not an answer, said God.

You're... you're like fire, dude, said Moses, in awe.

Moses, listen now. I want you to take your people out of Egypt.

We're not gypsies.

No, *Egypt!* The Israelites, Moses.

Right, yeah. Take em out. Bam bam!

No, Moses, listen. Take the Israelites out of Egypt to a land of milk and honey.

Sure, take them to Malcolm Manni... is he Mafia?

Listen you fool, hissed God (or the fire). I will give you a token.

Who will? said Moses.

I will.

Who're you?

I am that I am, said God.

So am I, man. We're like the same, you and me.

The hell we are! roared the fire, as lightning bolts and thunder and all manner of flames and suchlike fell about Moses.

Gah! screeched Moses leaping for cover: I'm falling.

It's called tripping, Moses, replied God, but

everything's okay now. I am your Lord.

Okay, said the shivering Moses, thinking that God was a comforting presence, like a warm fire on a cold desert night.

Now, said God, seeing that Moses had calmed down somewhat: Did you get that? Free my people.

Alright, I'll go to Egypt and bring the Australians to Malcolm Manni. Anything else?

Yes, tell the women to steal all the jewellery they can.

What?! Dude, that is messed up, said Moses. Wait, how do I know you're really God and that I'm not just tripping?

See that rod you are carrying, said the bush. Throw it to the ground.

Moses did so and it turned into a snake.

Hiss, said the snake.

Aargh! said Moses, leaping back.

Relax, said God, just take it by the tail.

Moses did so and it was once again a rod. He peered at it carefully.

Hmmph, well okay, I'm convinced now that I'm not tripping and that you really are God, said Moses, but he was talking to himself. The bushfire had gone, leaving Moses and the sheep and the mountain and the magic snakerod.

Dude, what about the token? said Moses to himself, but receiving no reply, he shrugged his shoulders and began gathering his flock.

Co-come on sssh-sheepysheep, he said, let's fly home to ma-mamabear.

From that day forth, Moses never again touched the weird desert plants (at least not in their raw format).

Moses' vision had given him the excuse he needed to get away from the seven sticky sisters, not to speak of a purpose hitherto lacking in his rich-kid navel-gazing lifestyle.

He returned to Jethro, his father-in-law, and said to him: Je-Jethro, I-I am go-going–

Why are you talking like that? said his father-in-law suspiciously. Wait a minute, did you eat those funny purple plants?

N-no, lied Moses. A-anyway, I'm away on a mission from God, a-and–

Oh thank the stars, said Jethro, you're leaving at last. You were no good at minding sheep and you've an appetite on you that would eat me out of house and home. Go, and do not return, and take your wife with you.

That was easier than I thought it would be, thought Moses. Brave old Jethro is concealing his sorrow well.

N-now, he said aloud, which one of you is my wife again?

At the sound of his voice, two sheep began baa'ing. One of the seven sisters put up her hand shyly.

Ga-great, said Moses. Le-let's get a move on. I'm on a mission from Ga-god.

His wife rolled her eyes – trust her luck to marry a holy Joe – but nonetheless, she gathered up her things, said her goodbyes and followed her husband to Egypt.

Moses had a brother in Egypt, Aaron. Unlike Moses, Aaron had never known what it is to be abandoned to die in the Nile by his parents, and enjoyed a carefree childhood and early adulthood with neither delusions of grandeur nor homicidal tendencies towards Egyptians. In order to slip back into the country, Moses sent word ahead to meet with Aaron on the outskirts of Egypt, under cover of darkness.

Seeing a figure approach, Moses took shelter behind a bush and called out.

Coo, coo, coo coo, he said.

Moses, is that you? asked Aaron.

H... how how did you know it was me, b-brother?

Well, I told you to make an owl call, because it's the middle of the night, and you did a pigeon.

A... and and how do you... knnnow the difference?

Aaron raised an eyebrow at his brother, but didn't deign to enlighten him.

So Moses, he asked, what's all this about, then?

Moses explained all that God had said to him, and the mission he had been entrusted with. Aaron observed Moses' stuttering and strange pauses in speech, and later noted also occasional fits, bouts of leprosy on his right hand and bursts of fierce aggression, and made a mental note never to touch the strange desert roots Moses made constant mention of. These side-effects left Moses disadvantaged in social situations and thus unable to eloquently lead his people to freedom.

S-so that's wha-why Gah-God wants ya-you as ma-my PR person. I'll ba ba... be the brains of the operation, and you... you you're to be the mouthpiece.

Hmmmph, said Aaron. Fine, if that's what the Lord wants.

In truth, Moses was suffering from occasional panic

attacks and hallucinations as well as stammering, since the eating of the plant. Part of him wondered if he wouldn't have been better off staying with Jethro, minding sheep and eating mutton every night. Nonetheless, with Aaron involved, it was too late to back out.

First up, they went to Pharaoh.

Ah, hello fellows, said Pharaoh. Let me ask you both a question: what did the Egyptian say to his friend after lashing the Israelite with the whip?

Aaron and Moses looked at one another, bemused, then shrugged.

Hebrews easily, said Pharaoh.

The Israelites did not laugh, and Moses wondered how much Pharaoh knew of his hidden past.

Relax, it's a joke, said Pharaoh. Now, gentlemen, time is money, so what can I do for you?

It's about the release of the Hebrews from slavery.

What about it?

We'd like it.

Whoooo, said Pharaoh, pursing his lips. You know, he continued grandly, as he reclined in his throne, if you had come to me two decades ago, guys, I'd have been delighted… only too happy, I would've been, truly. But in the meantime, we've converted the Hebrews from immigrant layabouts into a crack construction team. Have you seen what they're working on over at Pyramid Heights?

I have, nodded Moses. It's… it's a fine-looking development of townhouses and unique one- and two-bed apartments. Is… is it too late to—

Oh, I'm afraid so, said Pharaoh. Phase I is

completely sold out. Phase II is available from the plans, but we're awaiting funding from the Phoenicians, and–

Well the thing is, said Aaron to Pharaoh smoothly, sneaking a pointed look at his fool of a brother, we'd like the release of the Hebrews with immediate effect.

Like I was saying, Aaron, said Pharaoh, it's just not possible. Timing is everything, and we're in the middle of a construction boom here. If circumstances were different… He trailed off and spread his hands placatingly, before motioning for the next petitioners to be brought in.

Aaron and Moses saw that, for now, trying to make further headway with Pharaoh would be gambling with their own heads, so they left.

Hmmph, said Pharaoh, looking warily at the brothers as they left. He motioned an advisor forward.

Nehumtup, get the Hebrews working double-time on the overnight shifts. There are nefarious plans afoot, and we need to get Phase II at Pyramid Heights underway pronto, or the Phoenicians will call in the loans and I'll be sunk faster than a Sudanese dhow.

Naturally, the Hebrews began to grumble amongst themselves due to the increased workload.

This is all the work of that rabble-rouser Moses, they observed, and complained to Aaron.

Once more, Aaron and Moses went to Pharaoh.

Ah, the Hebrew Brothers. Do me a magic trick, said Pharaoh.

Aaron threw down his staff, and it turned into a snake.

Meh, said Pharaoh, waving his hand. At this signal, other enchanters and sorcerers entered and did the same with their sticks.

Now we have a room full of vipers, said Pharaoh, looking at the political advisors around him wryly, so what do we do?

Aaron's stick-serpent swallowed up all the other ones.

One magic trick does not an emancipator make, said Pharaoh. We shall meet again.

And with that, Pharaoh glanced at his sundial and swept out of the room to have his thrice-daily shave.

What on Earth am I to do about this reverse alopecia? Pharaoh asked his shaver. This five o'clock shadow is a nonsense.

There are hormonal treatments, his shaver replied carelessly, oestrogen and so forth, but really you're fighting your genes. Is it possible you might have some Greek ancestry?

Hah, good one, laughed Pharaoh mildly, then had the shaver killed once he had finished his task. If word ever got out that one of his forebears actually was one of those hairy Communists, the Hebrews would be the least of his worries.

The next week, Pharaoh was out on the Nile on his boat, when he saw a bedraggled figure standing on the shore.

Aaron, he said, is that you?

Let my people go, said Aaron.

No, said Pharaoh.

Behold, said Aaron. Let the waters turn red with blood, and let everything in the water die.

Following a slight delay (while Moses upstream was busy polluting the river with cochineal dye from a factory his cousin Nigel owned), the river turned red.

Who's paying for this? asked Nigel anxiously, watching his entire stock of dye slip away down the Swannee, one of the Nile's minor tributaries.

Gah-God, stuttered Moses, then pushed him roughly out of the way to initiate part two of the plan: throw dead fish into the river. He emptied buckets of them into the Swannee, and watched as the stinking fish flopped out and floated down to the confluence and into the Nile.

Back downstream, Pharaoh watched as the river turned bloody and dead fish populated the surface of the mighty river.

It's been done before, said Pharaoh, unimpressed. Sethkaphet the Sorcerer turned it green with creamy frothy bubbles for Paddy's Day, and Ankhemun actually turned it invisible once.

You mean he dammed it?

A magician never reveals his secrets, or so he said before he died, replied Pharaoh with a knowing look at Aaron. Now, can you get rid of that awful fish stench, he continued before reclining in his chair, because that would be a trick worth smelling.

Pharaoh's dhow picked up pace away from the smell of rancid flesh, leaving Aaron standing dumbly on the shore, gagging from the rotting fish.

D… did it work? asked Moses, breathlessly appearing

by Aaron's side.

No, said Aaron glumly. Ask 'God' to come up with something better.

Oh mercy, said Pharaoh when he saw, once more, Aaron and Moses before him. Who let these two in?

But Pharaoh was mock-serious; in truth, he hadn't had so much fun in years.

Why have you come before me? said Pharaoh, then mouthed the words as Aaron spoke:

Let my people go, said the leader of the Hebrews.

Always the same tune, Aaron; and always the same refrain. The answer is 'No'.

Right, well then, there shall be frogs everywhere upon the land.

Great, I love French cuisine, thought Pharaoh, but he merely replied: Please, no, not frogs. Nor snails.

Ha, said Aaron when he and Moses left. We have him now.

B... but where are we going to get that many frogs?

I know this weird fella that lives out on the marshes, Paul Bar-Simon, and he gathers frog spawn.

Fuh... for what?

God, I don't know, Moses. He's a strange man, they all are out there. Anyway, we'll take as much as we can get from him, then disperse it throughout the land of Egypt overnight.

And so it was done. Thirty-seven tonnes of frog spawn liberally applied to the waterways of lower Egypt and a week later the land was covered with frogs.

He'll be ready to give in now, wait and see, whispered Aaron to Moses as they appeared once more before Pharaoh.

Greetings, my Hebrew oppressors, said Pharaoh, as he snacked.

What are you eating? said Aaron, sniffing the air suspiciously.

Chicken wings, said Pharaoh disingenuously, humming a few bars of Le Marseillaise. Care to try one?

Yes thanks, said Aaron. Mmmph! God, those are good. What is that seasoning?

Paprika with some fennel.

It's delicious. Another? Why not, thank you. So Pharaoh, said Aaron, chomping down as many free chicken wings as he could manage, are you about ready to give in?

Hmmm, nearly. Alright then. If you get rid of the frogs, so that they remain only in the waterways where they belong, I'll let your people free.

Th… Thanks Pharaoh, said Moses, and they left.

That's brilliant, said Aaron. We just need to unleash the ten thousand barrels of snakes I bought, and the frogs will be gone in the morning.

And it was done, but Pharaoh still would not release the Hebrews.

Aaron went in a rage to Pharaoh, but he refused to see him.

Why not? demanded irate Aaron.

Because he does not like snake meat, replied Pharaoh's advisor pointedly, quite so much as he does frog's legs.

He smiled at Aaron without warmth. Aaron smiled back, cold as a leper's pinkie finger, then turned on his heel and left.

The advisor watched him depart and said to himself: Pharaoh is one psychopathic bastard, I'll give him that. I'd have just had you killed months ago, but he insists on toying with you.

You can't trust a word Pharaoh says, fumed Aaron.

Aa… ah, leave him be, said Moses. He's not the worst of them.

Who's worse than him, Moses?

W… well, Gah-God *could* just make Pharaoh let us go.

Aaron pondered this utterance of Moses in private later that night. He had a point, his mad fecker of a brother. It was difficult to understand why God didn't just whisk them away from Egypt, but then, perhaps being God meant you understood more of the ways of the world.

In any event, the next day, Moses had another idea. That is to say, God had another idea, and Moses was the channel.

Why doesn't God just tell me the idea? asked Aaron. There's a danger of something being lost in translation if you relay it to me, isn't there?

Qu… quiet you, said Moses, and an… li… listen.

He whispered in Aaron's ear the next plan, not even stuttering as he did so.

Really? said Aaron.

Moses nodded confidently. He had done his homework on this one.

Aaron called in his extensive contact list and got a barrel of pernicious lice from a fella who dealt with the jungle people from down South.

Is this good stuff? he asked him.

The very best. Or worst, depending on your perspective, said the trader, a sneaky-looking sort.

What's the cure?

Something higher up the food chain, said the trader. I should think flies will do it.

And you have them?

Boxes of them, grinned the trader through his crooked teeth, but they'll cost you.

How much?

Your first-born...

What?!

Eh, you didn't let me finish, said the trader quickly. I meant, your first-born's caul.

Why? That's sick.

I have a standing order from a northern witch in desperate need of such things, he replied. Deal or no deal?

Deal, muttered Aaron, but I'll have to go search in storage for that caul. Could be anywhere.

Second-born will do, so long as it looks authentic.

I have no clue what you're talking about, said Aaron, and he left the creepy trader's lot in the marshes and headed back to the sanctity of the downtown core.

By now, Pharaoh's stables and animals were overrun with lice, but repeated washing kept him relatively sanitary, so while he was miffed, he was not unduly concerned.

Aaron appeared confidently before Pharaoh in the midst of this lice epidemic.

So? he said.

So what? asked Pharaoh. You mean to tell me this lice epidemic is your doing?

It is God's work.

Fine, said Pharaoh, only it's you Hebrews that have the long hair and hairiness. We Egyptians, he continued, are unconcerned with such creatures as require hair or fur to adhere to. All our womenfolk are brazilian too, if you know what I mean.

I do not.

No matter. The lice are of no concern to us.

Nonetheless, faltered Aaron, trying his best to conjure a commanding voice, I will make the lice disappear.

Oh? Pharaoh's interest was piqued. He was always open to a magic trick he hadn't seen before.

Yes, look to the sky in the East on the fourth day hence, and I will free this city of lice.

Wait, said Pharaoh coldly.

Aaron froze, suddenly terrified. He turned back slowly to face Pharaoh, who wore an impassive look upon his majestic face.

Yes? said Aaron.

Remind me again, said Pharaoh, which one is East?

Where the sun goes at night, said Aaron with a surge of relief, and hurried from the royal palaces.

God dammit, he said, I'm getting twitchier than a ferret in a foxhole, and it's not just the damn lice.

He scratched his nether regions and determined to ask his wife if she had a brazilian like the Egyptian women.

He received a hefty whack across the jaw for his troubles.

Have you been carrying on with those whores? his wife demanded.

No!

You have, she insisted, that's why I have these itches.

No! You just have lice.

Another whack across the jaw.

How dare you, she said: I don't have lice.

You do; everyone does. I released lice upon the city.

You did what?

I released lice upon the city, to teach the Egyptians a lesson so that they will let our people go.

You total noddy, said his wife. You know lice only attach to hairs, right? And the Egyptians are the baldest people ever created? I mean, they are obsessed about absenting all their body hair. You do realise that, yes?

I just... it was God's idea.

That idiot brother of yours, more like. Isn't it time you did some real work for once, instead of ducking off pretending to be some sort of go-between for us and Pharaoh.

Darling, you don't understand; I'm the leader of my people.

I thought that was Moses.

He's just... I'm the real leader, and I'll show you, I'll show you all.

With that, Aaron stormed out of the house, shouting Slam! in lieu of an actual door.

Four days later, he stood on a hill crest to the East of Egypt in the early morning sun. He looked down across Egypt, as the calm of the morning gave way to a light breeze. Two paces further back, Moses wrestled a buzzing barrel onto its side.

Okay, said Aaron, it's time. Moses, when I raise my arms in the air, pull the plug from the barrel and kick it down the hillside.

Lo and behold, he cried. Pharaoh, look upon the Lord's work and fear his might!

Aaron raised his hands towards the sky. A pregnant pause followed, where nothing happened.

Now Moses, now! he hissed.

He turned to look. Moses had lost control of the barrel and was halfway back down the escarpment having finally halted it.

The Lord will unleash another plague upon Egypt on my count. In ten, said Aaron, nine… eight… seven…

He risked a glance back at Moses who was hauling the barrel back into position.

Six… five… four… three…?

Moses nodded and pulled the plug, grinning at his brother.

Two-one, tadaaa, said Aaron, as a loud and angry buzzing black cloud emptied from the barrel and was blown down towards Pharaoh's palace.

Haha, he said, *sotto voce*. That'll teach those bloody Egyptians.

After two days, Moses and Aaron were summoned before Pharaoh.

Excellent, said Aaron, we have him now. Normally

we're the ones knocking on his door.

Halloa Pharaoh, said Aaron cheerily, as they entered his chamber.

Look, these flies are a bloody nuisance, said Pharaoh, as a flunky swatted them away from the human embodiment of the Sun on Earth. What do you want me to pay you to get rid of them?

Thi... thirty talents of gol– began Moses, but Aaron shushed him.

I'll get rid of the flies if you let my people go for three days into the wilderness to pray.

Ah, like Woodstock? said Pharaoh. Done, but get rid of the flies first or no one goes anywhere.

You melon, said Aaron, with your thirty talents of gold–

You're the melon, said Moses, so furious he couldn't even stammer. We could pay exterminators for a month with less than one talent, then we'd have twenty-nine talents left. That would be more than enough to buy all the Hebrew slaves in the city, then we could have just left, with some money left over for ice-creams for the hot journey across the desert. Who's the melon now?

Aaron said nothing in reply, merely kicking a stone down the lane in sullen silence. After a long quiet walk, he finally broached the subject of ridding the place of flies.

Pe-pigeons, said Moses knowledgeably.

Pigeons?

Yes, pigeons. You know, coo coo, coo coo?

Yeah, I know what pigeons sound like, Moses. How many?

A… about forty.

Just forty?

Thousand, Aa… Aaron. Forty thousand.

Mother of God, said Aaron. I'm beginning to think my wife's right. This is hopeless.

Thi… this is not hopeless. Gah-God is on our side.

I wish he'd hurry up, said Aaron despondently; I'm running out of cauls to pay weirdoes with.

Aaron found himself in the marshes once more, holding conversation with yet another merchant of suspect character.

Pigeon-fancier, Aaron said to the merchant and his daughter. What is that exactly?

Well we– began the merchant's daughter.

The abridged version, the pigeon-fancier interrupted, giving his daughter a meaningful look mismatched with a sweet smile.

Are you okay? said Aaron to her. You look a little ill.

Well, said the daughter, it's just… sometimes pigeon faeces causes… well, epide–

The daughter was suddenly dragged into the backroom, before the fancier reappeared out front.

She's having a mild episode, he said. Don't mind her, or anything she said.

Oh dear, said Aaron, is she okay? How did she fall ill?

Oh you know, probably the lice or the flies. Know anything about that? the fancier asked.

Oh alright, grumbled Aaron. How much are these pigeons going to cost me?

Almost nothing. See they're homing pigeons, so

119

they'll all come back here in the end.

Great, thanks, said Aaron, turning to leave.

Wait! I said *almost* free.

Aaron turned and slapped a caul on the counter. That cover it?

How did you–?

Divine feckin intuition, Aaron muttered and stalked away from the bazaar.

Honestly, Moses, Aaron said to his brother, once we've got our people out of here, I'm through, you hear me? I don't want to have another thing to do with God. I mean it. Let someone else do all this monkey work. I'm fourscore-and-three and it's time for me to retire, settle down and draw a pension.

Ha, pension!? said Moses. Goo... good luck with that. You *have* no pension because you've never done a stroke of decent labouring work in your life.

Says the chief of the layabouts himself! retorted Aaron.

Fisticuffs ensued, and some kicking of the shins, but Moses and Aaron didn't stay angry with one another for very long, neither being able to stand anyone else's company.

About a week later, Aaron arose early, having had a fitful sleep. The air seemed poisonous and heavy; he stepped out onto the roof for a breath of fresh air, and immediately understood why.

The sky was black with pigeons, coo-cooing and flapping lazily about, munching as many flies as they could, then falling fatly to the ground, farting out gases and little pigeon poos from their excesses. By evening, most of them had returned to the fancier of the marshes, with a few of their number still lolling about in the squares, picking up tidbits from tourists, developing a new branch of the lineage in the process.

Aaron left it a day before he and Moses scuffled over to the Pharaonic residences.

Howzat Pharaoh, he said smugly, see how I got rid of the flies–

And brought a plague, Aaron, said Pharaoh. Pigeon dirt is highly toxic stuff and full of viruses and bacteria. Don't you know anything? All my hired labourers are off sick today on account of this mini-plague, so no one is going on their holidays anywhere. And my cattle are all coming down with something. They're dying in their hundreds thanks to those birds and their poop.

Not ours, said Aaron proudly. We use a pour-on disinfectant that makes the meat taste like medicine, but it keeps the bastards alive. Nothing can kill them.

Nothing? inquired Pharaoh.

Literally. We cut bits of them off and cook 'em, and the bits just grow back. I have a bullock that must be two-score years old if he's a day, and you couldn't tell him apart from one of your organic hand-reared yearlings. It's a fine thing they can't reproduce on account of the compromised sperm or they'd overrun the Earth.

Never mind that, said Pharaoh, although he made a mental note never to touch Hebrew beef stew again. Get the people back to work, and no national worker's holiday this year because of the mini-plague you caused.

Moses and Aaron left the court of Pharaoh.

Pe... people will be pe... pissed about National Worker's De... Day, said Moses.

Thanks Moses, I was aware of that, said Aaron acidly. Look, what are we going to do now? What does God suggest?

Te-time to roll up ma-my sleeves. I'll let you know ta-tomorrow, said Moses, and disappeared down a sidealley towards the spices and Eastern 'herbs' district.

He was out of ideas, but felt a hankering for that magical herb that had given him that crazy dream all those years before. Wandering down the dark dingy lanes of the cramped and muggy bazaar, he came upon an entrance. A small sign overhead the doorway said: *Best Desert Flowers and Plants, Cooked to Your Liking.*

He stepped in through the curtain over the threshold, setting the bells at the bottom tinkling, and found himself in a cool and dark place.

A small aged man shuffled out from a backroom.

Some spices, young man? he asked Moses in a strange accent.

One in par-particular, said Moses, from the Si-Sinai.

Blue roots. Green-yellow five-petal flower. Look like trumpet?

Ya-yes, that's the one.

You from secret police?

N-no, said Moses stoutly, Fa-fuck Fey-Pharaoh.

Indeed. Good. Okay, I have flower in back, in powder.

Oh, said Moses, a crease crossing his brow.

No worry, it's better. We add rosewater from clay well. It hundred-percent safe. Just take seat, he said, I come back.

He eased Moses into a booth with a reclining chair, then pulled a heavy curtain about him and hurried away to prepare the potion.

Within moments, he had returned.

Now, he said, roll up sleeve and relax.

Aah, sweet release, said Moses, settling back into the comfortable chair. Hook me up to God, he mumbled to the old man, who got him a clean line.

The next morning, Aaron discovered Moses lying in a heap of trash at the side of his house.

Wake up, you scoundrel, are you wasted?

Aaron, said Moses. God spoke.

Moses, said Aaron wearily, I'm sick of this shit. We had a chat last night, me and the wife. I just want to live out the rest of my days here. The healthcare is good, my bones are brittle – I'm blaming the pour-on disinfectant in the meat – I just don't want to do this anymore. Pharaoh is just jacking us around.

No! said Moses furiously, thrashing about the rubbish as he staggered to his feet. He grabbed Aaron by the throat and held him against the wall.

No, Moses continued: Listen to me, Aaron, I had my vision, and we're nearly there. It's going to get worse before it gets better, but the end is in sight. Nobody quits now, you hear me? No one.

Aaron fell back from this new man, seemingly rejuvenated by his vision, and apparently having undergone a complete change of personality.

Now, continued Moses, there's a bad weather front coming in tomorrow.

Bad?

Terrible, it's a combination of low pressure over the Sahara and unusual weather systems out over the Indian... you know what? None of that matters. We need to get to Pharaoh this minute and warn him of this. And by warn, I mean threaten.

Moses hustled past Aaron, and strode towards Pharaoh's palace. Aaron stood in amazement. He was terrified but enthralled. This new Moses did anger and action like no one he'd ever seen before.

Pharaoh was similarly impressed by this change in Moses, but remained resolute nonetheless.

All that night, and the following day, thunder and lightning and hailstones the size of thumbs were unleashed over all of Egypt, and the crop was destroyed in large part.

Pharaoh's advisors wondered if it might not be better to release the pesky Hebrews and get rid of them for once and for all.

Pharaoh raised an eyebrow at Nehumtup, his closest advisor: Really, Numty, what you are suggesting is mass murder.

No, you don't understand... said Nehumtup falteringly, you'd be releasing them–

Yes, into the desert with that fool Aaron. A man who can't tell his East from his West. Oh yes, Numty, I tested him before and he couldn't even do that much. That man couldn't find you a drop of water in an ocean, I'm telling you. He wouldn't last a day in the desert, and I'm not going to entrust the lives of the rest of them hairy brats to him.

So, keeping them here is an act of mercy?

Meh, it doesn't hurt that they are great workers and refuse to join unions, not like those micks we imported from the Barbary pirates. Bloody waste of time, that was. But no, I'm saving them from themselves. Or from Aaron, anyway.

Moses appeared before Pharaoh.

I have come to announce, he said, that if you do not let my people go, I will bring a plague of locusts upon the kingdom.

Locusts have a high nutritional value, said Pharaoh calmly, if one has the nets to catch them.

What?

Yes, they're a pest. Yes, they eat all the crops, but they convert that into a relatively nutritious source of protein. Better than cattle, in fact.

Pah, said Moses, storming off.

What did he say, asked Aaron of Moses when he returned.

He was terrified, said Moses, who had already paid for the damn locusts and was determined to use them in any case.

Haha, I bet he was, said Aaron gleefully. It was easier being second-in-command, and much more fun now that his brother had taken control again.

As Locustgate and the debacle over who would pay for it subsided, Moses arranged to meet with Aaron at one of the new restaurants that had popped up all across Egypt, serving up the insects 'any style'.

What's good here? Moses asked the waiter, after he'd arrived.

Chef recommends the Mediterranean fusion locusts, replied the server, and today we have some spicy deep-fried wings on special with beer.

Fine, said Moses. Bring us two specials and a plate of the traditional desert-style falcon. Now Aaron, he said, turning to his brother, what–

Excuse me sir, you want a side order with that?

Tabouleh and hummus, said Moses. Wait! Do you have kebabs?

Of course, pigeon or lamb?

Lamb, said Moses, thinking regretfully of the money wasted on the pigeons.

And how would you like to pay… ?

I wouldn't… Oh alright, gold shavings, but I'll need a receipt, said Moses.

Now brother, said Moses, after they found a table in the shade: I have a plan that will scare the life out of Pharaoh for once and for all.

Great, said Aaron.

Yes, he'll be properly terrified.

Nice work, Moses. Can I ask, what is it?

It is a mighty and horrifying occurrence to take place three days hence.

Oh, said Aaron, a worried expression furrowing his brow. Is it outdoors?

Yes…?

Well, you might have to delay it; there's a solar eclipse–

Who the hell told you about my plan? said Moses in

a furious whisper.

What?!

The eclipse; how did you know about it?

Well, there are government notices everywhere about it. Look, here's one right here.

Aaron plucked a flyer from the adjacent table.

> "People should not be frightened by the darkening to take place on Wednesday afternoon. It is a regular scheduled solar event that will last for approximately seventeen hours. Thursday will be similarly dark, and also Friday; however lanterns will be available from all good stockists."

Balls, said Moses, smashing his fist into the table, before things turned even worse for them.

A non-eclipse-related shadow fell across the pair. They looked up to discover two of Pharaoh's elite guards standing over them.

You, come with us, said one of them to Moses. Pharaoh has tolerated your rabble-rousing for long enough, but fears you have become radicalised.

Pharaoh?! Oh sure thing, said Moses, anything I can do for the boss. Let me just nip to the bathroom first.

Okay, but don't be long, said the second guard.

Might as well go too, said Aaron, slipping out from behind the table.

Ha, Hebrews, said one guard to the other. They have such tiny bladders.

They chortled merrily at the Hebrews with their tiny bladders, as Moses and Aaron wriggled out through the narrow bathroom window at the back of the restaurant and scarpered down the alley.

Gentlemen, said a server approaching the two guards, can I get you anything?

No, we're just waiting on these two Hebrews to come back from the bathroom so we can arrest them and bring them before Pharaoh, said the second guard.

Ooh, said the server, there's no one in that bathroom; I've just cleaned them and signed the roster sheet myself two minutes ago, if you're from the health board.

We're not, but bollocks! said the guards. Pharaoh is going to be so mad.

Aaron and Moses, meanwhile, realised things were coming to a head, so they gathered together all their people.

What's this all about, then? said one of the Hebrews.

Okay guys, said Moses. I have gathered you here today to release you from bondage.

The BDSM group protested, but were ignored.

That's not fair, they cried, we're a minority.

You're a minority within a minority, said Moses, so technically that makes you a majority.

No it doesn't.

Yes, it does.

Well, in that case, majority rules, they said, and cheered in victory.

This isn't a democracy, replied Moses. I'm the boss around here.

That's not fair, said one of the group. I know my rights.

I know my rights and my lefts, retorted Moses. Someone take him outside and have him clubbed to death with spears.

A civil-rights lawyer called out: Wait, that's not fair.

Quiet, you! said Moses. His temper was on a hairtrigger with the stress of imminent death by Pharaoh, and he still hadn't got to the crux of his speech.

Okay, Moses continued: As you all know, I've been busting my chops trying to get you people free, for which I have endured all manner of hardship. However, I am pleased to announce that Pharaoh has agreed to set you free.

Hurrah! cried the crowd.

Aaron looked strangely at Moses, who ignored him and said: Now, there are two things. No wait, three things. There are three things.

One. Pharaoh doesn't want this getting out, or they'll all want freedom – the Nubians, the Kushites, the Phoenicians...

A chorus of booes rang out until Moses silenced them by raising his arms above the people.

Okay, he said. That's number one. That's obvious. Now, number two. We'll need liquid assets.

The crowd were silent.

Beer? asked one, after the period of quiet grew uncomfortable.

No, not beer, you fool, spat Moses. Cash, jewels, silver, gold, precious stones.

I'm a minimum-wage worker, said one. I don't have any of that lying around.

Beg, borrow, steal, said Moses. Without some form

of it, you're not coming. Everyone's got to pay their way.

This sounds terrible. I'm staying, said one man, and he wandered off to seek an audience with Pharaoh and be rewarded for his loyalty. Moses nodded towards the quitter, and Aaron sent an assassin after him to reward him for his treachery.

The rest of the crowd were grumbling at this point, and one called out: What's the third thing?

What? said Moses.

You said three things.

Ah yes, said Moses, the third thing is God has spoken to me, and he has this to say: *From this day forward, none of our people shall eat unleavened bread.*

A hand shot up.

Joachim, yes? said Aaron, wearily.

Why not?

I knew someone would ask, said Moses, and the answer is this…

He paused, and the crowd leaned in.

BECAUSE GOD FUCKING SAID SO! roared Moses. IS THAT GOOD ENOUGH FOR YOU?

At this, babies began crying, women wailing and men shaking at the knees and hips.

Any more questions? barked Moses.

There were none.

Very well, he continued. Listen carefully: everyone is to eat grilled lamb cutlets tonight, and sprinkle lambsblood on your door, and lock them. Gather up all the valuables you can and get ready, because at first light tomorrow, we are leaving from the Eastern gate–

Some of you might know that as Marketgate, or the

Red Sea Trunk road, interjected Aaron.

—and going home, finished Moses.

He paused for the inevitable cheer, but there was none. People looked afraid and confused, and there was a hum of hurried conversations.

Home? queried one, a general merchant, aloud. This is home. My family's been here over four centuries. We pay our taxes, I have my own servants, healthcare, a pension, friends and family, business contacts. Why would I risk all of that for some scrap of desert no-one has seen for generations?

Moses tried to suppress his rage, but his stick failed him. It launched forth and smacked the fellow square on the bonce, sending him to the floor.

A spy, Moses screamed, a fucking Egyptian traitor! Any other such spies will meet with a similar fate. Now, get out of here, all of you. Bring jewels to the Eastern gate at first light tomorrow. The Lord God does not look kindly on traitors and spies.

He stared icily about the crowd, breathing heavily. Shying away from his terrible gaze, the crowd fled to break up their living accommodation and prepare for leaving behind all they knew and, if not quite loved, certainly tolerated.

Moses stepped off the dais and into the backroom, where Aaron and his crack commando unit were preparing for the night of terror.

Everything in order? Moses asked.

Sir, yessir, said Aaron, straightening up and clicking his sandal heels together: We have three squadrons, taking the East, West and North quarters.

What about the South? asked Moses.

Well, that's the Hebrew quarter, said Aaron, there's no need to kill the male children there.

Fair point, said Moses. Boy, is Pharaoh going to be pissed when he wakes up tomorrow morning.

Good enough for him, that bloody Greek, said Aaron, the racist.

The following morning, Pharaoh was woken by his advisors to learn that the Egyptians sons had been slaughtered by the Hebrews, who had furthermore stolen a considerable quantity of wealth and fled the city.

Goodness me, he said. This is terrible. Any idea where the Hebrew are headed?

Reports from the East gate state that a crowd of about six hundred thousand men, plus women and children, had gathered there this morning.

Did the guards there round them up?

No, well apparently the crowd's leader claimed they were heading to the beach for a picnic.

Seriously? said Pharaoh.

Apparently, yes, sir, said the advisor.

When did we become so gullible?

Well, sir, one might suppose that–

It was a rhetorical question! bellowed Pharaoh, then narrowed his eyes. Well well, Moses. You've gone too far now. Time for you to meet your end. Commanders!

Pharaoh's Joint Chiefs approached.

Sorry for the loss of your sons, said Pharaoh. Now, the perpetrators are headed for the Red Sea. Prepare the chariots and let's go to war.

A thunder of horse hooves and chariot wheels

heralded the departure of Pharaoh and his army from the East gate of Egypt, with glinting spears and shining swords and fancy armour. They were in a mood for vengeance, and headed towards battle with the Hebrews.

Up ahead, the crowd were snaking towards the Red Sea. Aaron and Moses, at the head of the throng, looked back across them. Luckily for them, Moses knew his East from his West, and they were making good time.

Moses, said Aaron, if Pharaoh comes after us with his whole army, we're screwed. Most of these people have no weapons. It will be a slaughter.

Don't worry about it, said Moses, setting his teeth and jutting his jaw forward determinedly. I have a cunning plan, and this time, it's going to work. We just need to push on to the Red Sea.

At last Moses and his people reached the glittering body of water. Moses peered into the sun and mentally calculated something as Aaron kept watch back towards Egypt.

A low rumbling and a tiny movement along the horizon indicated the approach of Pharaoh and his bloodthirsty vengeance-seeking army.

Moses, said Aaron anxiously. They're closing in on us.

We'll need to buy ourselves some time, as I suspected, Moses muttered to himself. Okay, Aaron, give the command to the people to tie rags about their noses and mouths, then set fire to the haybundles we brought, and fire those smokebombs I bought in the eastern bazaar.

In moments, a thick wall of dense smoke was created.

At the far side of this smoke, Pharaoh and his men furiously pulled to a halt.

Come, let us go through, said one of his commanders. It's just a smokescreen.

No, said another, that's exactly what the Hebrews want us to do. It's a trap.

Nonsense, said a third, they only want us to think it's a trap. Let's go.

Stop, you fool, said a fourth, don't you see? They want us to believe that it's not actually a trap, but only an illusion, and in fact–

Silence, all of you, commanded Pharaoh. They've reached the Red Sea, and unless they can walk on water, there's nowhere for them to go. We wait out the smoke and sharpen our swords for the slaughter.

Moses, meanwhile, keenly watched the Red Sea. At last, he nodded and said: Okay, it's time. Everyone forward.

The mass of people hurried forward towards the water, helped by prodding from Aaron's crack commandoes.

Aargh, the water's wet, cried one of the people.

We'll drown, said another.

Get a move on, said one of Aaron's soldiers.

Indeed the water was wet, but it was only up to their shins, and was receding.

In a curious location along the southern part of the Red Sea, a raised bank along the seabed allowed the Hebrews to rush across at low tide. When everyone had made it across, the men tending the fires and smoke bombs made haste to join the rearguard.

Once the smoke began to thin sufficiently to see what was going on, Pharaoh and his chariots burst through, wielding their razor-sharp weaponry.

Goddamn it, stop them! Pharaoh shouted. They're getting away!

The Egyptians hurried after the Hebrews, thundering forward onto the raised bed in their chariots; however, the horse hooves and chariot wheels pushed through the soft sand of the seabed and became stuck. Simultaneously, the tide returned. With further chariots and horses shoving forward into the churning water from behind, panic ensued. Pharaoh's army was decimated, then decimated again, and again, and again, in an iterative function, until only Pharaoh was left in the middle of the Red Sea, atop the tallest horse.

Woe is me, he said, as the water splashed against his chin, and after all I did for you people, too.

He took a final breath of air and then, with a rueful gritting of his teeth, said: Good luck with those Wahhabi bastards in Saudi, Moses.

The waters rushed over his head and he was no more. Another god for the afterlife.

Across the water, the Hebrews looked back and were overjoyed.

Hurrah, they cried. Hurrah for Moses. Hurrah for God. Hurrah for the end of Pharaoh and his army.

They sang and shouted *Hurrah* until they grew hoarse

and hungry, about three minutes later.

Who brought sandwiches? someone asked.
Oh God yeah, said another, I'm famished.
And a beer to wash this sand out of my throat,
rejoined a third. Hey Moses, where are the beers?

Moses did not answer. He was up ahead with Aaron,
looking across the vast, searingly hot, inhospitable
wasteland he had brought over half a million people to.
Not a scrap of vegetation, nor a drop of fresh drinking
water marred the view of bleak and barren misery. A
lesser man than Moses would have wept. Moses merely
gritted his teeth, spat in the face of this unspeakable
hardship and turned to his brother.

Aaron, said Moses, I think our little adventure is only
just beginning.

Find out what happens next to Moses and his Crazy Gang. *The Holiest Bible Ever: Rise of the Sherpa* is coming soon.

To stay up-to-date with new books in this series and our other publications, join our mailing list – mail@westclarewriters.com (We will only email when new books are released. Pinky promise.)

In the meantime, gorge yourself on these tasty offerings from the West Clare Writers Collective:

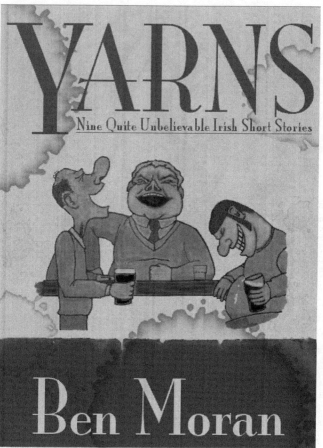

Soaked in spirits and drizzled in mist, **Yarns** is a collection of real short stories set in the fictional land of West Clare. Or fictional short stories set in the real land of West Clare. That is to say, don't believe everything you read. Cute hoors abound, not to mention greyhound-tamperers, amorous octogenarians, first-time fishermen, snickering clergymen and nocturnally-vigorous undertakers; everything Bórd Fáilte would love to advertise (but legally can't, for fear of appearing to condone this sort of thing).

Yarns also contains *The Author's Guide to Tracing*, including correct usage of the *Nyeh!* (not to be confused with either the *Yerrah!* or the *Sure!*)

ALLERGY WARNING:
Contents include coffee, coffins, squirrels, muffins, greyhounds, graveyards, turf and tractors. (Also crossbows.) May also contain suspect morals, 'colourful' language and observations on life as it is lived out west. No added sugar.

THUMB PRINTS

Short stories by
Lou Shalloo

Thumbprints features twelve stories of modern life in and around Dublin, of people from many walks of life; some following the road chosen for them by others, some carving out their own unique path, all making choices that are at once personal and universal.

The stories centre on those private moments when we converse with ourselves, alone: the thoughts we dare not share, about those closest to us, about the true cost of success, of struggles with duty, and what might still be possible at the far end of failed relationships.

Also peeping over the horizon:

The NSA.

When General Whiteley is appointed interim head of the USA's disgraced intelligence agency, it seems a matter of time before it is shuttered forever... only no-one told the General. Thus begins the greatest fightback in the entire history of human civilisation...

Or does it? The General and his right-hand man, Alfred Smugh, must battle hostile Senator Carolyn Bigsley, President Meeke, the Administration, and someone within the Army... not to mention the Dread Bearded Terrorists, dodgy accounting practices, misappropriation of funds and corporate joint-ventures with certain hamburger-selling multinationals.